1980

PATHWAYS for the POET

PATHWAYS
for the
POET

POETRY PATTERNS

EXPLAINED AND ILLUSTRATED

BY

VIOLA JACOBSON BERG

mott media
BOX 236, MILFORD, MI. 48042

LIBRARY OF CONGRESS CATALOGING IN
PUBLICATION DATA

Berg, Viola Jacobson, 1918-
  Pathways for the Poet.

  Bibliography: p.
  Includes indexes.

  1. Poetics.   2. Versification.   I. Title.

PN1042.B47   808.1   77-4357
ISBN 0-915134-18-7

FOR

The see-ers and visionaries of tomorrow,
the students and aspiring poets
who desire to see beyond scrub pines
into the beauty of the forest,

The teachers of today
who encourage creative minds,

The lovers of poetry
whose appreciation strengthens the poet's noble role,

with the prayerful hope
that this book will give
blessing and inspiration.

CONTENTS

PREFACE

In our day the term poetry is loosely used. To one person it may connote what to another is mediocre verse. All true poetry, however, exhibits three basic characteristics: worthy content, beauty in some form, and skilled craftsmanship. For the work to be unique, a fourth quality — originality — must be added.

Poetic technique is a living, evolving craft. This book defines and explains various tools and patterns available for the poet-workman. It is only an introduction. The developing poet will wish to continue further in his own research and study. (See Appendix I: Helpful Publications.)

Pathways for the Poet is primarily a collection of over two hundred of the patterns for which explanations and examples are available. Much of this information can be gleaned from the many "how-to" booklets on the market, especially those offered in little poetry magazines. This book assembles them into one practical reference guide. Its unique feature is that all of the examples of the patterns, including those from the 17th, 18th, and 19th as well as 20th century, have been written by one poet.

The section devoted to "The Poet's Tools" includes detailed descriptions of rhyme and meter, and brief definitions of other techniques such as various figures of speech. Although it is not necessary to master this material before going on to the section on "Poetry Patterns" — for mastery comes with practice — it would be wise to study these tools carefully. Before starting out on a walk, it is well to know the nature of the pathways.

The patterns include traditional forms, rhymed and unrhymed, from the English, French, Asian, Italian, Japanese, and others, as well as modern American forms not included in poetry encyclopedias to this date. Some, therefore, are gifts to us from antiquity, such as ballads and sagas, enjoyed before the invention of the printing press, and the centuries-old haiku. Others will take their own place and receive the recognition they also deserve for their contribution to beauty.

The content of the poems in this book covers a wide range, from dandelions to world brotherhood. Some of the materials reflect my faith. Faith is a vital part of my life, and I write about spiritual themes just about as naturally as I breathe. But I have selected only those inspirational poems which I feel, for one reason or another, have a right to be here. I have purposely used a comprehensive variety of subject material with the hope that, apart from the mechanics which are given concerning the examples, the poetry itself will offer enjoyment.

Also it is my joy to contribute some new forms of my own and to present them in this book. To the best of my knowledge, after extensive reading and study, I could not find any instance where these patterns were used by any other poet. If another writer has written in the identical form at some time or another, the occasion would be a coincidence for these patterns have evolved from my own extensive creative writing experience. I use the term "introduce" rather than "originate" in presenting my forms, and trust they will bring pleasure to those who use them.

The illustrations used in this book vary in quality as well as content. Because we are complex personalities and creatures of many moods, we do not write at the same levels of feeling and excellence at all times. A number of example poems have been kindly judged to be worthy poetry by discerning critics. Most of the material pretends to be nothing more than acceptable verse. Some poems have never gone through the screening of an editor's discerning eye. Here and there among the contents, however, is sprinkled a prizewinner. The poetry examples in the book represent a cross section of life as experienced by one person.

The explanation of the patterns has been kept to a reasonable minimum. An involved explanation might lead the struggling beginner to think that writing the form is more difficult than it is. It has been proven that the easiest way to learn to write in a form is by studying the example, reading it aloud if necessary to get the swing of the poem as a whole, and then concentrating on the rhythm, line by line.

I trust the reader will be challenged to try these patterns. Start with the simpler ones and work into the longer, more involved ones. (Use the guide in Poetry in the Classroom: For Teachers.) Watch yourself grow and develop as a poet, and enjoy the fulfillment and satisfaction which will be your reward.

That is the whole idea — to get you writing — and I hope you will have a wonderful time in the many pathways of your choosing in your pursuit of poetry.

Every effort has been made to find the originators of the forms presented in this book. I want to thank every one of our modern poets for the contribution they have made and are continuing to make to the poetic culture of our day. Thanks are also due to the editors, librarians, and fellow poets who have cooperated in the painstaking detective work of tracking down the originators of these beautiful patterns. Sincere thanks is especially due Miss Clara Gates, poet–editor–librarian, for her perseverance and help. It is the desire of the author and the publisher to give credit where credit is due. If any oversights have occurred, it has been in spite of all our efforts, and not from lack of trying.

I must also thank posthumously a number of the poets of the past, as their forms are among the most loved and beautiful patterns in the book.

ROLE OF THE POET

To reach to hearts by phrase and word
That mutual voices might be heard:
The joy of spirit loosed and free
Reverberates in poetry,
For souls must reach if they would fetch
A treasured dream, some gold to catch
To share with those who lost their star
And guide them where the wishes are.

—VJB

WHY WRITE POETRY?

POETRY–THE ESSENCE OF LIFE

Poetry is the essence of life packed in a golden thimble. Poetry is a perfume that invades the sensitivities of the soul.

Poetry is the joy of laughter, the tears of heartache, the agonies of disappointment, the wonder of love, the fulfillment of understanding, the miracle of communication, the tangible expression of the language of the heart.

Thomas Carlyle writes: "Poetry is the universal language of mankind, in which all men link their hearts and minds in understanding."*

Poetry is far superior to prose in emphasizing the force and effect of a thought, the richness of a concept, the cleverness of an idea, the delicacy of an emotion, the purity of feeling. It is the essence of life in all its facets — compacted, captured, displayed.

Consequently to write poetry is to experience more excitement, more challenge, and more joy than is to be obtained from other types of writing. A poet gives more importance to sounds, to mood, to connotation. He uses rhythm, rhyme, and form, if he so chooses, to make his writing pleasurable to the ear and eye. Somehow by combining whatever he desires of figurative language and even something as fanciful as whimsey, he can bring forth part of his own mystical inner self, and reach out to the mystical self of another.

*In *Paths to Parnassus*, Stella Craft Tremble (Charleston, IL: Prairie Press Books).

Inside the hearts of most of us is a longing to retain the treasure-nuggets of our own life's experiences. To capture in words the emotional experience of the moment or the apex of past highlights is a pleasurable and effective way to hold on to and savor those moments of awareness, of contemplation, of inner searching, of beauty, of exaltation, of suffering, of joy. And all that is needed is a pad and pencil.

BENEFITS

Let us consider a number of benefits directly derived from the writing of poetry.

It may, for instance, provide relief in a poignant situation. What an outlet for an outpouring of joy, sorrow, nostalgia, disappointment, or hope! The impelling desire for expression can be so strong, so overpowering, that to let the pen run its gamut is truly and actually a relief.

When a poet shares his heartache and his tears and gives tangible form to his grief, the sharp edge of their sting is somehow dulled. The gnawing ache is miraculously lessened as his sorrow is shared with the readers to whose inner consciousness he mysteriously appeals. The writer and reader are bound together in a soul-broadening experience, causing both to savor the preciousness of life and the fellowship of love.

The exercise of writing poetry can sometimes open doors to unexpected delights. It is a common misconception that unless one's poems are widely published and one is literarily successful, one has failed. This is not so. It is very possible to win a mental laurel wreath for one's own private creativity which could not be bought for all the money in the world, for inner joy is not available for a price. Fostering one's creative potential can build self-respect and confidence in a most engaging way.

In these days of much deviousness in politics, situation ethics, and surface social niceties, it is a relief to be honest. Basic foundation honesty provides a release for the spirit. The poet, using the unique combination of frankness, impelling desire, and freedom of spirit, can communicate his intensity of emotion to reach other inner selves of the universe. It gives a largeness to life, a widening of the doors of the soul.

What an ennobling experience to discover what is beneath the superficial camouflage of our personalities. It takes depth to reach to depth, and only out of the depths can one achieve the terrible authenticity which gives writing its conviction. By writing poetically the writer can experience to the full what he finds in the inner recesses of his being. He does not lose what he finds, but savors it, captures it, shares it.

Writing poetry gives the freedom to be completely original. Only you can write your poem. In one sense, no one can criticize it, for it is a unique creation, bigger and more intense than our ordinary selves. We draw from the world of our own "beyond-ness." In exposing and capturing our own personal responses, especially if we incorporate a measure of expertise in the writing, we can communicate through the magic of a poem.

Who hasn't appreciated beauty in some form, at one time or another — maybe a breath-taking sunset across the bay, a stand of graceful pine trees silhouetting a ridge; or maybe it came through the medium of sound, the glories of Beethoven's *Moonlight Sonata.* Each such experience aroused such intense response that one actually ached to hold onto it, loathe to let such beauty go. How can anyone gaze upon a perfect rosebud without realizing his own incapacity to absorb all that perfection? However, there is nothing to stop any of us from attempting poetically to capture that sense of wonder.

WHERE WORSHIP IS COMPLETE

Where hide the words I long for
To frame a summer day?
To capture magic's heartbeat
And store my dreams away?

The secrets of the breezes
Are hid from grasping mind;
A probing, dancing sunbeam
Will never be defined.

The charm of smiling rosebud
Is not in line or phrase;
The spirit aches with longing
To capture wonder's gaze.

The magnitude of moonglow
Bows not to mold of men;
The symphony of sunrise
Is not in poet's pen.

The world of purest feeling
Which language cannot greet
Is only for the reverent
Where worship is complete.

Why write poetry? Why not? The effort in itself repays with a more integrated personality, a heightened sensitivity of one's own worth, and the incalculable worth of all of God's creation.

To someone who would really like to write, but who is not inclined to turn his heart inside out to do it, there are rewards also for the creator of light verse. It is fun to incorporate humor, whimsey, a touch of the ridiculous, a play on words, a pun or two, even some irony and satire.

Backed into a corner at a social affair, the captive audience of a dogmatic, self-opinionated bore, can give vent to an outburst like this:

PARDON MY YAWN!

We all need reminding
To welcome fresh thoughts,
A hint which should not make us huffy,
For a mind that is shut
Like a room that is closed
Can become quite unbearably stuffy!

INSPIRATION

An aspiring poet might long to experience the joys of writing but his well is dry. I suggest in that case that he prime the pump, that he give his natural creative processes something with which to work. One cannot force inspiration. It must come from a natural spillover of the emotions, convictions, desires, and urges from within.

One who lives fully will want to write fully, who loves deeply will wish to share the magic in his writing. For the music lover, the full enjoyment of delightful harmony and rhythm provides fragrant hyacinths for the soul. Contemplating an inspirational article or a psalm, studying uplifting poetry (not one's own), are other proven ways to prime the wellspring of the heart. A phrase or a connotative idea is very apt to spark the imagination (to change the figure), and the poet will find himself reaching for his pencil. The impelling desire was there all the time, but the sensitive spot had to be touched to release it.

And what an area for the poet to share his faith! Can anything be closer to the heart than the personal relationship with God and the lessons He teaches? As the poet seeks to share the way out of a valley time, the lessons obtained through experience, study, or tears might wonderfully bless, help, and encourage the reader in his own valley.

A little serious contemplation will reveal endless areas of subject material. Memories can be very rich: the smell of the honeysuckle, the memory of the pink hollyhocks blooming by the gate, the crackling campfire at the cookout, the haunting sunset in the desert, the magic of awakening love and the thrill of that first kiss of long ago, the voices of loved ones who have long since gone to sleep. And the poet won't want to stop, even if he could, for he has tasted that which only a creator knows. He has given life, pulsing and throbbing, to that which has been touched and awakened in him.

PATTERNS

Poetry forms are simply patterns. Just as a tailor would not start cutting into expensive suit material or a carpenter begin sawing into a piece of rosewood without knowing that all the pieces would fit and the result would be harmonious, neither should a writer expect a lovely well-crafted poem to emerge unless he adheres to accepted characteristics of excellence. Even a person with a mild interest in writing poetry should be familiar with the traditional forms and make an honest attempt to write them.

The benefits of writing in established patterns are many. An ordinary quatrain can take on a professional quality by expertly adapting it to a traditional form. It can be set off to advantage, just as the beauty of an oil painting is enhanced when it is placed in an attractive frame. Do not underestimate the value of form. It not only adds dignity to the poet's efforts; it also gives the writer versatility.

The writing of free verse, which does not require meter or rhyme, is, nevertheless, very demanding. A foundation in all the basics of poetry will automatically make an aspirant a more effective writer of free verse. In addition, the mental exercise involved in following rhyming schemes, counting syllables, and making every word work, is excellent training for the serious writer of all kinds of quality prose.

Each form has value, for its very uniqueness is challenging. From the imitating of each form will come an intrinsic broadening of the writer's vocabulary and a strengthening of his poetic skill. Developing a poetic approach takes time, experience, and diligence. There are no short cuts to the eventual writing of that poetic gem.

The ultimate goal of any aspiring poet is to have a collection of his writings accepted for book publication. The editors who decide which books are of lasting value and literary merit will be bored with your labor-wrought brain children, no matter how beautiful the actual content, if after a few pages, all they have seen is sing-songy verse in common meter. Diversification and mastery of various forms and styles must command and maintain the editor's interest before he would consider underwriting the expense of publication.

When I taught a "Fun with Poetry" course at a private high school my students had to learn all the fundamentals before they progressed to the fun part of the course. They were taught how to write in all the meters; they learned the intricacies of rhyme and the many ways in which it can enhance a poem. They were introduced to the various intriguing tools of the poet — alliteration, assonance, cadence, connotation, metaphor, parallelism, consonance, pathetic fallacy, all types of imagery, refrain, sound and sense, and so on. Mastering all of these techniques did not make them poets, but it helped tremendously to shape their natural talents so that each one of them was able to create a poem worthy of publication.

A WORLD WITHIN

In each of us there dwells within
A power to tap through discipline,
And as we search with joy we find
The great potential of the mind.

The creative joy of writing poetry, however, cannot be contained. It is bigger than any of us, which adds to its excitement and its mystery, for if a person can experience all that he can imagine, words at best can only express a part. Yet each of us has the privilege, the wide-open opportunity of trying. But let me add this word of caution. He who earnestly seeks for the alluring and irresistible company of the Muse will be unable to retreat. She will never let him go. This delightful poetic world with its many pathways, its fascinating doorways, and its mystic rewards may overwhelm him, but he will stand at a keener threshold of awareness, to pause, to contemplate, and to wonder at the potential that has come to life in him.

IN PURSUIT OF POETRY

In reaching for a melody,
A tune we hear, but do not see,
Which somehow cannot be contained
But only felt, its sweetness pained
For lack of proper labelling
Of definitions which but bring
The aspirant to know that he
Will never conquer poetry,
But rather in pursuit of it
It conquers him, till bit by bit
He somehow feels his soul expanding,
Eluding human understanding,
To then decide with thankful heart
Simply to enjoy the art.

*The following poems appeared in *For Kindred Hearts* by Viola Berg (London: Mitre Press, 1976): "Pardon My Yawn," "Where Worship Is Complete," "In Pursuit of Poetry."

GETTING PUBLISHED: FOR POETS

So you would like to see your poems published? You are one of a hopeful multitude of thousands. But this dream does not have to be shelved as impossible. This wish comes true every day for those who take their prized poems from their secret hiding place, who believe that those efforts represent something which would interest others, who dare to expose those efforts to the review of an objective editor, and who follow a few simple rules and ethical procedures.

SUBMITTING MANUSCRIPTS

If you hope to have your poetry receive due consideration, then it is imperative that you know how to type (or can hire an able typist). Editors want clean, freshly-typed copies on standard business-size white paper. The name and address of the writer should appear in the upper left hand corner. A self-addressed stamped envelope (SASE) should be included for the convenience of the editor's reply. Unless you include the SASE, he is not obligated to answer you. Editors are sensitive, discerning, and usually overworked. They receive stacks of unsolicited material every day. If your poem looks attractive on the paper (double-checked for misspellings and typos), it will get its turn for a fair amount of the editor's attention. Your poems should be enclosed with a brief, polite cover letter. If you know the editor's name, then address it to him.

Start at home in your community with local newspapers and magazines. The fact that you are a resident will help your chances of being published, especially if you write on a subject of current local interest.

If you decide to venture further, most of the denominational and interdenominational religious magazines use inspirational poetry. Take careful note of the type they use. If you have something which you feel would fit into their categories, then go ahead and submit. The only way to get started is to make the first move.

Before submitting material to any type of magazine, study editorial requirements from the listings in the writers' markets. Know as much as you can about what the editors are looking for, from whatever sources are available, before you submit. Much postage and time can be saved, and much disappointment avoided by being very selective and wise in submitting. At the current cost of postage (especially since you must enclose a SASE), it is more important than ever that we slant our writings and our submissions, using our best judgment and sending only our best poetry.

A writer has a greater chance of having a poem accepted if he sends three or four at a time, each on a separate piece of paper, containing varying content and written in various forms. This will give the editor a choice. Short poems stand a better chance than long ones. Many publications do not accept poems over thirty lines; some only twenty, sixteen, or even less. Some editors make their decisions purely upon the impact of the poem. (See Appendix I: Helpful Publications and II: Market Listings for poetry outlets.)

For your own peace of mind and so you will know at a glance where your materials are at all times, you should develop a system for record keeping. Always keep carbon copies of all materials submitted; note the date of submission and to whom they were sent. Keep a file of information on three–by–five cards, one for each publication with which you deal, noting on this card the titles of the poems you send. This will prevent confusion in future days when you are considering re-submitting. Record all responses on the card. If you have an acceptance, congratulations! Except for extenuating circumstances, that poem is not to be resubmitted elsewhere. You are free, of course, to submit unaccepted material to another editor. Keep careful record of your accepted poems and any monies received. It is to your own benefit to be businesslike in your bookkeeping.

Do not send the same poem or group of poems to more than one editor at the same time. Never send the same poem purposely to the same editor twice, thinking he might like it better the second time. He won't. And do not send submissions to the same editor at close intervals. Every three months is acceptable, since many publications are quarterlies. Submission of seasonal poetry must make allowance for advance planning. Allow six months.

REASONABLE EXPECTATIONS

You will not make much money writing poetry. Even established poets who have had a number of books published do not depend upon the income from writing for their support.

The major outlet for the work of poets, especially beginners, is poetry magazines. Most of them are not in a financial position to pay for the works they accept, and are largely dependent upon the subscriptions of their contributors to stay in print. These editors are warm, wonderful people who offer their time and talents, and in some instances subsidy, to keep these publications going. They add immeasurably to the poetic culture of our day, and deserve the support and cooperation from those who need their outlets in order to get started.

Some publications pay well if offered exactly what they are looking for. But these checks, even for the seasoned poet, are the exception rather than the rule. Resign yourself to the inescapable fact that if you want the satisfaction of seeing your work in print, you will have to give most of it away.

The occasion of the acceptance of your first poem is a red-letter day in your life, as it should be. You have earned the right to run up a flag or two. But in a very realistic sense, it is a private victory. Your husband–wife–children–relatives–friends cannot fully understand the extent of your own elation. But do not allow what seems to be inadequate appreciation from those nearest you to dampen your own enthusiasm. When they become used to the idea and are ready to share your interest more fully, they will let you know. It is wiser and more acceptable to underplay your role than to indulge your irresistible urge to poke your latest prized poem under their noses. Recognition, even with one's family comes slowly. If you have the persistence to stick with your interest, and you continue to get acceptances, your family will gradually realize that they have a writer in their midst. You might even be given a ream of paper or a box of envelopes for your birthday instead of a box of candy!

social life, but the writer part of himself — the world of his own "beyondness" into which only he can enter. His sense of isolation, though self-imposed, and the lack of empathy he may sometimes feel are a part of the writing experience. Such a situation is neither sad nor unique to writers. Don your writer's hat as inconspicuously and graciously as possible. The joy of creation is yours, and you have set your foot on the pathway!

However, if rejections piling up on your desk discourage you to the point of quitting, then this business is not for you. In writing, as in anything, bulldog tenacity, constant application, and patience are necessary to success. If your poems are good and you believe in yourself, keep sending them out. They will never have a chance for publication if you keep them home in a drawer.

If they are rejected repeatedly, some rewriting may be necessary. Perhaps you need a fresh slant or a better end line, even a more attractive form. Then send it out again with a new face.

If an editor is kind enough to give suggestions for improvement, profit by such criticism. The editor knows more about what he is looking for than you do.

On the other hand, editors are as variable as people. Quality requirements are of varying degrees, in poetry journals as well as magazines that use poetry. It is encouraging to know that we do not have to write prizewinners to have our work accepted. Of course, if a new writer wants to go beyond the first levels of acceptance, he must raise the quality of his writings.

Sometimes there may not be anything wrong with the poetry, but it just may not fit in with the format of the publication, or the editor may be overstocked with material.

Be realistic. Realize that not everything written is necessarily of lasting value. A well known modern critic has said that among really excellent poets only about one poem in fifty will live on after him.

Rather than be discouraged by such an evaluation, we can realize that in order to be able to write that occasional one poem of genuine merit, we are getting training and invaluable experience as we write all those in-betweens.

While waiting, write something new.

CONTENT AND PRACTICE

Anyone who has ever tried to put two lines together knows that the most important ingredient in good writing is content. Does the poet have something worthwhile and interesting to say? Much of modern poetry is pessimistic, cynical, sometimes morbid and even crude. Although one must write what is in him to write, it is this writer's opinion, shared by many editors, that one of the foremost responsibilities of the poet is to uplift, to benefit the reader. Dwelling on life's evils and rolling in the gutters to display naked realism for shock value does nothing in itself to cure these problems. Not that we should write with a pollyanna philosophy. Nothing could be so insipid as a steady diet of sweetness and happy endings. We need strong, virile, dynamic poetry, too, but of the kind that will challenge and stir the reader to constructive action.

The poetry which finds the most ready acceptance is written about every day things with which the reader can identify. Poems about ordinary happenings in an ordinary day can be presented with a fresh twist and a new approach.

Sincerity is a quality which cannot be manufactured. In order to produce such poetry, you must capture the idea when it is fresh. You then have the best chance of getting that spontaneity into your poetry.

In addition to these impulse writing episodes, which can come at any time (even in the middle of the night), you must seek out regular times of quiet and solitude. Most dedicated writers just cannot write without it. Expressing one's self with clarity and sensitivity just cannot be accomplished effectively when distractions break the train of thought. After a nerve-jangling interruption, more than likely you will find that your mood is broken and the words will not come.

A measure of success will come sooner if the writer does not take himself too seriously. Ideas and their tangible revelation — words — are best expressed by a mind which is relaxed and free to enjoy the unfolding creative process.

Beyond diligent application, most writers need the encouragement and understanding of others who share the urge to write. Investigate the creative writing classes in your area. Through the instructor or a fellow student you may be introduced to a local writers' group. Belonging to such a group may give you the boost you need and open many challenging doors.

Whether or not you seek for additional encouragement and guidance, do learn the techniques of self-appraisal. Some amateur poets are very dogmatic in their evaluation of their work and are over-sensitive to criticism. They may become quite indignant at the presumptuous suggestion that they change one word of it. An earnest poet will gladly spend the time required to find that vital perfect word, that elusive phrase or fitting verb. He will be eager to improve, rewrite, and polish. Very few writers (and this includes the old masters) are so good that they have no need to improve upon their first drafts. Cutting, tightening, and deepening will intensify the essence of your message. So be objective about your own work, for in pruning comes the excellence for which you strive.

Traditionally the role of the poet is a noble one. He can use his pen as a light to make the path ahead a little brighter. How refreshing his work would be if he would follow the suggestion of the Apostle Paul in Philippians 4:8:

> Finally, brethren, whatever is true, whatever is honorable, whatever is just, whatever is pure, whatever is lovely, whatever is gracious, if there is any excellence, if there is anything worthy of praise, think about these things (RSV).

POETRY IN THE
CLASSROOM:
FOR TEACHERS

How to write poetically can be taught successfully at all grade levels. Sometimes younger children are the most responsive.

But there is a difference between teaching students to write poetically and expecting them to write poetry.

The teacher sets the stage, instructs and indoctrinates, shares much information and inspiring examples, and encourages with genuine interest and excellent ideas.

But it is the student who must combine the ingredients of worthy content, beauty, skill, and originality to create the poem.

HELPFUL IDEAS

- Be enthusiastic. If your students sense that you are genuinely interested, they will respond accordingly.
- Try yourself to write every form you give as an assignment. There is no better way to prepare for student questions and to be able to give helpful suggestions.
- Impress your students with the untapped potential for creativity in each one of them.
- Include reading of teacher-selected poetry along with the writing assignments, both in class and for homework. This activity will stimulate ideas.
- Be sure your students know how to use a thesaurus; having rhyming dictionaries available.

■ For younger students, have the class create a composite work. Write the lines on the blackboard as the poem evolves. Hold out for a worthwhile idea and an interesting beginning. Show them how to lead up to a strong last line. The results might not be a literary gem, but if they had fun doing it, they will feel more confident to write on their own.

■ Students need much encouragement. Find something to compliment each one about before offering criticism on assignments.

■ Sponsor class, department, or school contests. A competitive challenge can be a great stimulus.

■ Do not expect too much, depending upon grade level of course. The work of some students will delight you; others will find this type of creative writing extremely difficult. Each student is different in natural aptitudes and talents.

■ Do not do their revisions for them, no matter how strong the temptation. Teach them how to scan their own poems for weak spots and how to improve and polish.

■ Do not limit yourself to this book. Many aspects concerning the writing of poetry are just touched upon or are not covered at all.

■ Students with special interest could receive extra credit by researching and reporting on such areas as:

> How to select a title
> Ways to judge between poetry and verse
> Selecting the exact word: shades of meaning
> The deeper language of imagery
> Fun with onomatopoeia

On high school and college levels the topics could cover larger areas and become more involved. For example,

> History of the French forms
> History of the haiku and other Japanese forms
> Variations of the sonnet
> A study of blank verse in literature
> The emergence of free verse in the last two decades

EVALUATION

Here is a simplified checklist for grading poetry. You may choose to present this to the students for their own use, but the knowledge should not intimidate. They should be encouraged to let their ideas flow naturally. Freshness and spontaneity can do more for a poem than lines contrived to impress.

> sufficient substance
> clear meaning

Septanelle
Sevenelle
Sonnet
Spenserian Stanza
Stellar
Stephens
Swinburne

Terza Rima
Thorley
Trench
Trianglet
Tribute Poem
Trilinea
Trillium

Troisieme
Tulip
Uta
Veltanelle
Violette
Virelet
Zenith

GROUP 4

Abercrombie
Balance
Ballade
Ballade With
   Double Refrain
Bragi
Caryotte
Chant Royal
Dionol
Double Ballade
Duni

Kerf
Kloang
Laurel
Manardina
Margeda
Marianne
Medallion
Metric Pyramid
Quintette
Rondeau
Rondeau Redouble

Scallop
Serena
Sestennelle
Sestina
Taylor
Tennyson
Triad
Villanelle
Wavelet
Zanze

THE POET'S TOOLS

RHYME

Rhyme is an ornament to decorate sound, to make it attractive to the ear. It must not be depended on to make a poem, but to enhance it.

Many adults retain a misconception carried over from childhood that everything that rhymes is a poem. Two rhyming lines can be just a bit of doggerel. Two unrhymed lines can be pure poetry.

Correctly used, rhyme gives a natural effect. If the lines sound contrived, earlier lines may need to be rephrased so that the rhyme-pair will enhance, not ruin, the sense.

Rhyming should be unobtrusive in serious poetry. However, obvious rhyming can be used to advantage in light verse, especially in limericks.

The natural order of grammar should not be twisted in order to accommodate rhyme, for then rhyme becomes the master and not the tool.

In the mechanics given for poems in this book, letters represent rhyming schemes, and numbers represent syllable count. Therefore, all "a" lines rhyme with each other, all "b" lines, all "c" lines, and so on. Lines for which no rhyme is required are designated with "x".

TRUE RHYME

The rule for a true rhyme is simply that the consonant preceding the accented vowel must be different. The endings must be identical in sound. Words may be spelled alike or differently. It is the sound that matters. Examples of true rhymes are:

> aid/braid/afraid/cavalcade
> blue/through/do/rendezvous/stew
> key/be/tea/agree/simile

Eye rhymes, words that look alike in spelling but are pronounced differently, are not rhymes. Examples:

> cow/snow; climber/timber

Hackneyed, trite, and obvious rhymes are undesirable. Examples:

> kiss/bliss
> love/dove
> trees/breeze

Identities do not rhyme. The preceding consonantal sounds must differ. Examples:

> see/sea; be/bee
> word/reword; plant/implant

MASCULINE, FEMININE, TRIPLE RHYMES

When rhyme is used in a poem, masculine rhymes are always paired with masculine, feminine with feminine, and triple with triple. The accent must always fall on the same syllable in relation to the end of the line.

Masculine rhymes are one–syllable words, or words of more than one syllable in which the accent falls on the last syllable. Examples:

> lap/nap/handicap
> eat/elite/street/parakeet

Feminine rhymes are words of two or more syllables, with the accent falling on the syllable preceding the final one. Examples:

> baker/forsaker
> baring/wearing
> mother/other/brother

In each **triple rhyme** the third syllable from the last is accented. Triple rhymes may be made up of more than one word. Examples:

> narrative/declarative
> tastefully/wastefully
> kind to me/blind to me

END RHYME, INITIAL RHYME

The following lines illustrate the use of rhyme at line beginnings (also called **head rhyme**) as well as at the end (also called **tail rhyme**). This example has been written in rhyming pairs.

PERFUME OF A MEMORY

> Breezed is a faint perfume,
> Teased by the roses' bloom,
> Lifting its scent to me,
> Gifting a melody.
>
> Oh, I could store away
> Glow for another day.
> Then when the bloom is dead,
> When skies are gray instead,
> I could reclaim delight,
> Cry for the magic sight,
> Filled with a deep content,
> Thrilled by its wonderment.

For other examples of initial rhyme, see "Ode to William Shakespeare" in the ARABESQUE pattern; and of initial and end rhyme, see "Parade of the Hours" in the CARYOTTE pattern.

INTERNAL RHYME

Internal rhyme is the repetition of the rhyme sounds within the line, or woven inside the structure of the poem itself. In each stanza in this example the first and third lines use internal rhyme. This effect is pleasing to the ear and enhances the rhythm.

IT'S FUN TO DREAM

> It's fun to dream of pink whipped cream
> Adrift on a chocolate lake,
> Of custard pies with cherry eyes
> And caramel icecream cake.

It's fun to fly through the tinselled sky
    And loop the loops with a hop,
In a ruby ship with a diamond tip
    And land on a lollipop.

It's fun to glide with the magic tide
    In a sailboat just for me,
Where sunbeams play and the mermaids sway
    To the beat of the waltzing sea.

What fun to be at a pixie tea,
    And sip from a bluebell cup.
But it always seems in my choicest dreams
    That my mother wakes me up!

For other examples of internal rhyming, see "My Bit of Sky" written in the KIPLING pattern; and "Nevermore," an example of PARODY.

HIDDEN RHYME

Hidden rhyme is a form of internal rhyme in which a word within a following line rhymes with the end word of a preceding line.

TO THOSE WHO ASK

When you are burdened with your care
And long to share your heavy task,
Just raise your eyes up to My face,
I give My grace to those who ask.

CHAIN RHYME

In chain rhyme the last syllable of a line is repeated as the first syllable of the next line. The repeated syllable, though having the same sound as its predecessor, must carry a different meaning.* Noun and verb forms have different meanings, and may be used to forward thought.

IN THE SPOTLIGHT

How fresh the day when it is born,
Borne to its destined call,
Calling the world to note its claim,
Claiming the eyes of all.

*Alex Preminger, ed., *Encyclopedia of Poetry and Poetics* (Princeton: University Press, 1965), p. 112.

38

RUNOVER RHYME

Runover rhyme pairs the last word of one line with the first word of another. Unlike chain rhyme, it is the rhyming sound which is "runover" and not the word.

LOVE IS ALL THE TIME

I love you in the dawning,
Yawning a bit, tis true,
But still I am intending
Spending the day with you.

What else may be in season,
Reason or writ or rhyme,
Hearts were made for sharing,
And caring is all the time.

CONSONANCE

Consonance is usually defined as the identity of the final consonant sound, or final unaccented vowel and consonantal sounds, but not of the accented vowel sounds. Example:

pillow/yellow
cradle/griddle

At times consonance refers to the repetition of the consonant sounds before and after the accented vowel. In this poem, the last words of lines 1 and 3, and of lines 2 and 4 show consonance.

NIGHT BLIZZARD

The freezing, numbing winter night
Reigned with pale moon mocking,
Staring, taking distant note
And lonely shadows making.

Helpless were the field and lake,
Wild life sought for cover,
Naked trees and wind alike
Whined till night was over.

With the dawning came the sun,
Through the blizzard shredded,
Scanned the icy scene and soon
Found the world enshrowded.

In another variation, only the beginning consonants may be paired and the vowels and ending consonants left unmatched. Again, notice the final words of each line in the example poem.

A CHANCE TO LOVE

I lifted my heart in the dark of night,
I offered my soul in the dawn of need.
In answer I felt an angel's kiss,
Was bolstered in faith by a voice so kind.

Oh, why do the stubborn grieve and weep,
And why do the helpless moan and wail,
When aid will come to those who cry,
And God will prove He is not cold.

He only asks for a chance to love,
He will not force His care and light.
When He is asked to guide the heart,
He proves His power to soothe and heal.

ASSONANCE

Assonance is the repetition of the final accented vowel sound without repetition of the surrounding consonants. Examples:

show/groan/soap/pole/told
red/hem/nest/tell/went

In this example the vowels are paired in alternating lines.

TRAIL OF HEALING

I speak, and words fall from my careless lips
Which often hurt, and I am unaware
That my inflection and ironic twist
Can turn what could be sweetness into ash.

But once the arrows tear the target raw
Those barbs will not retract, for they have dug
Into a tender spot, to wound, to haunt.
Too late I know my words have turned to dust.

Oh, tongue, unchecked as tide upon a flood,
Exploding over trifles to disgrace,
If used instead to speak kind words of love,
Could leave a trail of healing in its wake.

Rhyme, as seen in the many devices described above, is really a sound ornament that creates a musical effect by combining vowels and consonants in various patterns.

METER

Because there are so many manners of expression and word arrangement, various meters are needed to encompass the natural rhythms of speech.

Meter describes the sequence and relationship of all the stressed and unstressed syllables in a line, the arrangement of beats into a regular measured pattern. Each group of beats is called a "foot."

Conformity of beat is necessary to produce smoothness, but over–emphasized regularity produces monotony. On the other side, too much freedom can ruin the rhythm and destroy its appeal.

The table below lists the usual metric feet with name and description, number of syllables per poetic foot, example, and accent pronunciation. **Stressed syllables** are marked with (-), **unstressed** with (⌣). Poem examples written in each of these meters will follow later.

METER AND METRIC FEET

NAME OF FOOT	SYLLABLES	EXAMPLE	ACCENT PRONUNCIATION
Iamb (⌣ -)	2	aware	ta-TUM
Trochee (- ⌣)	2	mother	TUM-ta
Spondee (- -)	2	blackboard	TUM-TUM
Dactyl (- ⌣ ⌣)	3	butterfly	TUM-ta-ta
Amphibrach (⌣ - ⌣)	3	enjoying	ta-TUM-ta
Anapest (⌣ ⌣ -)	3	in the dawn	ta-ta-TUM
Paeon			
1st (- ⌣ ⌣ ⌣)	4	freedom to be	TUM-ta-ta-ta
2nd (⌣ - ⌣ ⌣)	4	the sky has turned	ta-TUM-ta-ta
3rd (⌣ ⌣ - ⌣)	4	in the prime of	ta-ta-TUM-ta
4th (⌣ ⌣ ⌣ -)	4	out in the great	ta-ta-ta-TUM

Less usual metric feet:

NAME	SYLLABLES	ACCENT PRONUNCIATION
Pyrrhic (⌣ ⌣)	2	ta-ta
Tribrach (⌣ ⌣ ⌣)	3	ta-ta-ta
Molossus (- - -)	3	TUM-TUM-TUM
Amphimacer (- ⌣ -)	3	TUM-ta-TUM
Bacchius (⌣ - -)	3	ta-TUM-TUM
Antibacchius (- - ⌣)	3	TUM-TUM-ta
Ditrochee (- ⌣ - ⌣)	4	TUM-ta-TUM-ta
Choriamb (- ⌣ ⌣ -)	4	TUM-ta-ta-TUM

NAME	SYLLABLES	ACCENT PRONUNCIATION
Epitrite		
class 1 (⌣ – – –)	4	ta-TUM-TUM-TUM
class 2 (– ⌣ – –)	4	TUM-ta-TUM-TUM
class 3 (– – ⌣ –)	4	TUM-TUM-ta-TUM
class 4 (– – – ⌣)	4	TUM-TUM-TUM-ta

Meter is given by numbers of poetic feet per line. These are referred to by the following names:

NAME	NUMBER OF METRICAL FEET
Monometer	1
Dimeter	2
Trimeter	3
Tetrameter	4
Pentameter	5
Hexameter	6
Heptameter	7
Octometer	8

Iambic pentameter, then, is five poetic feet of ta-TUM's per line. Trochaic tetrameter indicates four TUM-ta's. Dactylic dimeter would be composed of lines of two TUM-ta-ta's. The directions for metrical feet given in the patterns are determined in this manner.

IAMBIC METER

Iambic meter is the most widely used and the most natural to write. Each pair of syllables (⌣ –) is counted as one iambic foot. Thus a pair of five iambic feet (pentameter) would have a rhythm like this:

ta-TUM, ta-TUM, ta-TUM, ta-TUM, ta-TUM

The example poem is written in tetrameter and trimeter alternating. The first line will, therefore, have four stresses; the second, three.

GHOSTS WHO NEVER DIE

When blows the haunted tumbleweed
  I think I hear the sigh
Of phantom riders from the past,
  The ghosts who never die.

What tales the restless wind could tell
  To tear the bravest eye.
I only know when twilight falls
  I sense the days gone by,

And try to grasp its secret song,
To understand its cry,
But lassoed is the mournful wail,
Corraled to muted sky.

But even if its lonesome dirge
Will always mystify,
I feel the breath at twilight time
Of ghosts who never die.

TROCHAIC METER

In trochaic meter (− ◡) each line ends with a feminine word because the last syllable is unstressed.

APRIL BONNET

April is my darling's bonnet,
Brim of buds with fresh green faces,
Crowned with dancing sunbeam graces,
Kiss of velvet breeze upon it.

Ribboned apple blossom veiling,
Edged with daffodils beguiling,
Violets shyly peek through smiling,
Scent of dew-kissed lilacs trailing.
Joy of springtime rests upon it,
April is my darling's bonnet.

DACTYLIC METER

Dactylic meter, a three–foot meter, (−◡◡) is delightfully rhythmic. The last foot in each line of this example poem is **catalectic** (incomplete). The stressed syllable is present, but the rest of the foot is missing.

FAIRY FLIGHT

Butterfly, butterfly, dance through the air,
Magical flight of the breezes to share,
Find the camellias and lilacs in bloom,
Sway on the blossoms and breathe their perfume.
Visit the tulips so stately and tall,
Greet pansy faces and smile at them all.
Rest on a sunbeam in gay rendezvous.
I wish I could fly through the garden with you.

ANAPESTIC METER

Anapestic meter also has three syllables to the foot (ˇ ˇ −). Each line in the example poem contains three anapests.

FEATHERED REQUIEM

Every bird in the forest at dawn
Hushed its song, curbed the notes on its breath,
For its melody could not go on,
A wee robin had dropped to its death.

A mere fledgling had tried out his urge
To examine the wide world below,
Now the breezes blow softly the dirge,
For he fell in the morning's first glow.

All his friends brought a blanket of bloom,
As they pecked out a grave, warm and deep,
And their wave was like feathered perfume
As they left their friend robin to sleep.

AMPHIBRACHIC METER

This is a less usual meter of three syllables (ˇ − ˇ). This example has two complete amphibrachic feet in the first and third lines of each stanza. The second and fourth lines are catalectic. Part of the impact of this poem is the result of the skillful use of meter.

THE HEART-TUG OF YOU

A step in the hallway,
A breath on the stair,
And for a brief moment
I thought you were there.

Time gradually eases
My sorrow and then
The wound of my heartache
Is laid bare again.

I thought I'd forgotten
The heart-tug of you,
But then without warning
Your memory steals through.

A step in the hallway,
A breath on the stair,
And for a brief moment
I thought you were there.

SPONDAIC METER

Spondees ($--$) are often found in compound nouns such as "moon-light" and "sunbeam." They also occur when two strong one-syllable words adjoin. This meter is used in harmony with other meters to enhance a poem. In the first three lines of this example the spondees will be identified. Six more spondees are scattered in the balance of the poem.

LET THERE BE LIGHT

Twilight wraps the world in growing dark
As a mighty blindfold on our sight.
Every bright star with its pinpoint glow
Proves a cheer and comfort in the night.
Dawn's rays offer promise from the sky
To chase away the imprint of the deeps.
Landscapes long for gentle mute caress
Of phosphorescence, smiling as it sweeps
Across each waiting doorstep with its might,
Obeying God's command, "Let there be light!"

THE PAEONS

In four-syllable metric verse there are four positions for the stresses: first, second, third, and fourth. All paeonic verse, no matter where the first stress falls, sounds very much alike, for the only basic difference in the paeons is found in the number of unstressed syllables occurring before the first stressed syllable. The practiced ear can discern secondary stresses between the main stresses, shading the paeonic toward the iambic or trochaic. However, as the examples illustrate, it is much more rhythmical than two-syllable foot verse.

Since paeonic meter, by its very structure, is a fast meter (it fairly gallops across the page), this rhythm would not be chosen for a stately or dignified treatment of any subject.

FIRST PAEON (— ◡ ◡ ◡)

FREEDOM TO BE FREE

Freedom to be understood and freedom to be kind,
Free to turn from evil and to live with peace of mind,
Free to look beyond myself, to search, to climb, to dare,
Free to choose a nobler path, to seek for purer air,
Free to ask forgiveness, and to know that God loves me,
Freedom that will always last is freedom to be free.

SECOND PAEON (◡ — ◡ ◡)

HIS EYE IS ON THE SPARROW

The sky has turned to silver, and the clouds are tinged with blue,
The trees are tall behind me, but the sunbeams trickle through.
I've crossed a range of mountains and a river's sandy bar;
The right road leads to heaven, to my left an evening star.

I really don't know where I am, and yet somehow I do,
For I am in the Father's care, and, brother, so are you.
I'm far away from paths I know, but mercy's I still share,
God's stars keep right on shining, and His love is everywhere.

THIRD PAEON (◡ ◡ — ◡)

BEWARE

In the prime of early evening when the stars come peeking out,
When the moon is shyly beaming, then Sir Cupid is about,
Shooting each and every arrow from his bow with practiced art,
Letting fly his magic potion as he pierces through the heart.

So beware of moonlit evenings with their effervescent glow,
For that prankster hides in shadows and he's flitting to and fro.
So if you are idly flirting and you don't intend to stay,
Then by all means shun the moonlight, for you'll never get away.

FOURTH PAEON (◡ ◡ ◡ —)

HOW GREAT THOU ART

Out in the great wide world of nature there are miracles to see,
Out in the chapel of its magnitude, its Maker speaks to me,
For in its mountains and its forests and each awesome waterfall,
In every mighty surge of tidal wave, each redwood reigning tall,

46

There is a doubt-dispelling atmosphere which lifts above the sod,
Causing each eye to turn to heaven, and each heart to turn to God.

ADDITIONAL TOOLS

The following pages contain brief explanations for an additional
number of poetic tools given in alphabetical order. Most of these
devices are also illustrated; for some you will be referred to poems
elsewhere in the book. Though some devices will not be used extensively in writing, knowledge of them will be helpful.

A number of these terms deal with figurative language and imagery. Imagery is suggestive rather than exact, bringing out the
poet in the reader as well as in the writer. Images heighten every-
day language, add color to the pale, illuminate the dull, and intensify the ordinary.*

ALLEGORY

Allegory is described as the art of double meanings.** Abstract
concepts, such as Faith, are given flesh by making them into
characters or elements of nature. Unlike other figures of speech,
allegory is an extended narrative or poem, so that character and
action both tell a story and reveal a spiritual or philosophical truth.
The Pilgrim's Progress by John Bunyan is an allegory in prose.

FOREST FIRE AFTERMATH

Burned and gone beyond the scope of memory,
Your face receded past the grip of pain.
Yet the fire is vivid in the darkness,
And in the embered woods, the seedlings stir.
Under charred disfigured bark, remembering
The sap still runs with hope of sprouting green.
Conflagration forced all life to silence,
And yet somehow bold sparks invade my brain.
What is real, and what is but illusion,
And where is proof of fatal burn and scar?
Lightning streaks its murmurs in the darkness,
And in the deep of midnight, you are flame.

For another example, see "Time of Sheaves," a SEDOKA–
HOKKU; and "The Price of Harvest," a DIONOL.

*The Pursuit of Poetry, p. 59. Copyright © 1969 by Louis Untermeyer. Reprinted
by permission of Simon and Schuster, a Division of Gulf and Western Corporation.
**Untermeyer, Pursuit, p. 145.

ALLITERATION

Alliteration is the repetition of an initial sound, usually a consonant, in two or more neighboring words or syllables. For example,
"wilt and wane" from "To See the Light," DOUBLE BALLADE;
and "brave and bold" from "Katchoo!", a BREVEE. One of the
most familiar examples of alliteration is from the nursery rhyme,
"Peter Piper picked a peck of pickled peppers." The repetition
of the initial letter of the key words can weave a most magical
spell.

Another aspect of the use of alliteration is the repetition of the
same word at the beginning of each line.

In the following illustration the second stanza alliterates the first
word of the seventh line of the first stanza. The first word of the
seventh line of the second stanza then repeats the alliteration of
the first verse, thus tying the two verses together. Alternate lines
rhyme.

SOFT AS A WHISPER

Soft as a whisper of spring,
Soft as a kitten's low purr,
Soft as a butterfly's wing,
Soft as the memory of her.
Soft as the patter of rain,
Soft as the touch of a kiss,
Rare as the absence of pain,
Jewels too precious to miss.

Rare as the truth to embrace,
Rare as the dream that comes true,
Rare as the prodigal's face,
Rare as the absence of you.
Rare as the loves that we earn,
Rare as the season's first rose,
Softly the lessons we learn
Comfort when nobody knows.

The alliteration of this next illustration is a bit more subtle —
the repeating of an idea rather than sounds. The many colors
pictured here recreate the author's experience for the reader.

OCTOBER WOODS

I went for a walk in the woods today
To loose my mind from its somber gray,

And the golden sun on the speckled elm
Severed my soul from its somber realm.
The gleaming pond in this orange-lit scene
Had ripples of turquoise and blue and green.
The rusts and scarlets on bush and tree
All vied with each other to dazzle me.
The tints all around me renewed desire,
For who can be blue with the woods on fire.

CADENCE

Cadence, as its name suggests, is measured, rhythmic sequence of beats. Poetry composed in strict meter is characterized by its even flow. Trochaic meter is said to march; dactyls dance; and so forth.

The following poem is a striking example of marching rhythm. The format aids in forming the beats.

FORT GORDON, U.S.A.

March!	March!	March!	March!
Now	I know	what my feet	are for,
As back	and forth	goes the	army corps,
For a sol-	dier marches	forever	more
To the beat	of the big	bass drum,	bum, bum,
To the beat	of the big	bass drum!	
Br–r–um!	Bum!	Bum!	Bum!
We've only	been drilling	since half	past three,
But it seems	at least	an eter-	nity,
And now	my feet	are driv-	ing me,
As they follow	the beat	of the drum,	bum, bum,
As they follow	the beat	of the drum!	

CONCRETE POETRY

With a little planning and thought, poems can be arranged into the typographical shape of the subject matter, appealing to the eye as well as to the ear and mind. This poetic oddity is not new, having been employed through the centuries for serious poetry as well as light verse. Herrick's "To Christ on the Cross" is built in the form of a cross, and Herbert's "Easter Wings" is so spaced that the verses become a pair of tapered wings.*

*Untermeyer, *Pursuit*, pp. 133-34.

The examples show shaped items of light verse.

KING OF THE ROAD

How well do I remember the cars of other years, the isinglass for windows, the grinding of the gears. Those patched and daring tires, the spoke–filled narrow wheels, the high–arched dented fenders, the engine grunts and squeals. Washboard jars and jiggles, home folks taking wing, Dobbin's in the pasture, Henry Ford was king. Modern cars so shiny never hold for me, the three of spirit's flying   in
memory's   Model "T"

A TREE IS A FRIEND

A
tree
is a friend,
whom I
recommend, who
in summer will
quietly aid.
It whispers and
wheezes and plays
with the breezes and
gives me such
wonderful shade. It won't
run away. Its feet hug
the clay, a sentry who guards
for no fee. It has chloro-
phyll breath, and won't talk me
to death. Yes, a valuable friend
is a
tree.

CONNOTATION

Connotative meaning is the suggested meaning of a word rather than the specific definition, or **denotation**. Its meaning is derived from the emotional and other associations attached by the reader, the poet, and the culture, to that word.

This example poem uses words with rich romantic appeal.

ON SUCH A NIGHT

Soft is the night, so smoothly azure moonbeams
Kaleidoscope like rainbows through the trees.
Mysterious the gentle kiss of evening,
On waltzing flight of lilac scented breeze.

On such a night forgotten are the shadows
As gypsy spells pervade each starlit gleam.
A cherished voice reechoes in the stillness
And captured is the magic of a dream.

ENJAMBMENT

This term describes the running over of a sentence from one verse, couplet, or line, into another. It is the opposite of an **end-stopped line** which has a distinct pause at the end.

This example is from "Through the Snow."* For other examples, see "The Prodigal," a SONNETTE; "Blow, Bugles, Blow," a SPENSERIAN SONNET; and "Valley Rendezvous," a LUVAILEAN SONNET.

Through cold and snow they walked to find the house
Of God, then laid their flintlock muskets down,
Removed their hats and shawls, and sat alert
On rough hewn benches, stiff and straight, and hard.
But there they met their God. No Indian-threat
Could keep them home the first day of the week.
Too much they had endured to forego this,
The chance to worship as their conscience taught.

*See BLANK VERSE for entire poem.

HYPERBOLE

A figure of speech, a hyperbole is an extravagant exaggeration which a poet uses to give force and intensity to his statement. This example is from "Elegy to the American Legion."*

> Graves cannot contain their spirits,
> Halt their feet from keeping time.

INVERSION

Used poetically, inversion is a reversal of the normal word order. Generally considered inferior versification, it can be used for emphasis or to create a mood.
This example is from "Ballad of the Bedouins."** See line 6.

> There once was a father, El-Farid, his name,
>   Who lived far beyond the Red Sea,
> And he had a daughter, a sweet little daughter,
>   And a bright little gypsy was she.
>   . . . . .
>   Oh, play the lute sweetly, give ear to my song,
>   And blow, desert breezes, my story along.

METAPHOR

Although metaphor is one of the most essential figures of speech, it is the most difficult to define. It is usually defined as an implied comparison of two dissimilar things. The poet sees a point of likeness between two otherwise very unlike elements, and lets one stand in the place of the other to point out that similarity and to heighten the reader's awareness. The simile is a similar figure of speech.
This example is from "Another Day Unfolds."***

> Another day unfolds before my eyes,
> The hours, precise and silent, filter through,
> Each one for me a challenge and a prize,
> Each one a virgin in its mute debut.

An hour is likened to a precise, silent virgin making her debut. Notice that, more subtly, hours are compared to rays ("filter through").

---

*See ELEGY for complete poem.
**See BALLAD pattern for complete poem.
***See CHAIN VERSE for complete poem.

For other examples, see "When Tulips Bloom," MEDALLION; and "Snow Birds," SPORTS POETRY.

METONYMY

Another figure of speech, metonymy uses a feature or characteristic of a thing to stand for the thing itself. It may also use a part to describe a whole.

For example, "the deeps" stands in place of "sea" in these lines from "Out to Sea."*

> Too soon the ebbing tide will roll
> And lure me to the deeps.

In "Stampede of the Long Horns," from SPORTS POETRY, "feet" represents "team members."

ONOMATOPOEIA

The sound of some words suggests the meaning. This delightful tool causes the reader to hear, as well as to feel and see. The following simplified example illustrates:

BARNYARD CHORUS

> The cows are singing bass notes
>   as they raise their heads and moo,
> The hens are clucking alto to their brood,
> The mourning doves sing tenor
>   with a harmonizing coo,
> The pigs squeal high soprano for some food.
>
> The sparrows chirp and twitter
>   a ditty of their own,
> A pony whinneys forth his melody,
> The dog is adding volume
>   with his barking baritone,
> The ducks are quacking happily off-key.
>
> What a racket, what a babble,
>   as the turkeys add their gabble,
> The gander honks, the mule starts to bray.
> Then the rooster adds his crowing,
>   so I think that I'll be going,
> And listen to their music — far away!

*Quoted in full under OCTAVE.

OXYMORON

An oxymoron, a type of paradox, is a phrase of apparently contradictory terms, such as poor millionaire, happy mourner, cruel kindness. It can be used to describe the indescribable or the complex.

For example, "pathetic toys" in "Monarch of the Night," CANOPUS pattern; and "pained relief" in "Snow Birds," SPORTS POETRY.

PARADOX

A paradox is a seeming contradiction which expresses a deeper truth. Because of the nature of spiritual truths, for example, many are expressed in paradox.

For illustration, these lines from "Sympathy Becomes A Crown":*

> Only as we bruise and break
> Can we soothe another's ache.

Or this, from "To Keep Our Brother":**

> We listen, yet we have not heard,
> We see, and yet are blind.

See also "Journey of the Soul," a RHYMED CINQUAIN.

PARALLELISM

Phrases, words, or ideas can be repeated in a balanced format. The Psalms and Proverbs provide excellent examples of parallel structure and thought.

For an example of parallel structure, see "Morning Star of Day," THE ARNOLD pattern; and "Parade of the Hours," a CARYOTTE. For parallelism of both expression and structure, refer back to "Soft As a Whisper," under ALLITERATION.

PATHETIC FALLACY

Ruskin invented this phrase to describe the poetic habit of attributing human emotion to inanimate objects.

For example, "kind veil" from "Ballad of the Bedouins," a BALLAD pattern; and "tired rocker" from "The Little Country Things," a KYRIELLE.

*See MINIATURE pattern.
**See THE BLUNDEN.

PERSONIFICATION

Like pathetic fallacy, personification attributes human characteristics to abstractions or things not human. Since it is an implied comparison, it is also related to the metaphor.

From "Abandoned"* comes this figure:

> Deep within a hidden valley
> Waits a little church in tears,
> Left alone with only memories,
> Keeping vigil through the years.

For other examples, see "Monarch of the Night," CANOPUS; and "Rain," TANKA.

REFRAIN

The refrain is a phrase, a line, or lines repeated at intervals throughout a poem, often as the last line or lines of every stanza.

In "Ballad of the Bedouins,"** for example, every stanza ends

> Oh, play the lute sweetly, give ear to my song,
> And blow, desert breezes, my story along.

For other examples, see BALLADE, BALLADE WITH DOUBLE REFRAIN, DOUBLE BALLADE, RONDEAU, TERCETS WITH IDENTICAL REFRAIN, and TERCETS WITH VARYING REFRAIN.

SIMILE

The simile is really a metaphor that is a stated rather than an implied comparison. It often uses the introductory words "as" or "like," but will also be found with "than."

In "Soldiers on the Roof,"*** the raindrops are "like ten-thousand soldiers marching." From "Upon Our Doorstep"**** comes this comparison:

> A new born day is like a fertile field.

*See DECANNELLE.
**See BALLAD.
***See BLANK VERSE.
****See OTTAVA RIMA.

SOUND TO SENSE

The ideal poem is a delicate harmony of message and method. A melancholy mood is produced by playing on the conscious and subconscious with words that both sound sad and suggest sadness. The awakening of nature in spring must be vibrant with action verbs which breathe and tingle.

Two examples will be given to show the relationship of sound to sense. The first poem uses a combination of rhyme and consonance in its line endings, creating a certain aura of dissonance which complements the somber mood of the poem. The first and third lines are paired consonantly, and the second and fourth lines are rhymed in the conventional way.

SWORDS TO PLOWSHARES

The victims of the war, their bodies still and cold,
   Rest in sleep, but unseen spirits roam.
Our vibrant sons the enemy has killed
   Search in their dreams for home.

They do not know death is a gentle friend,
   From hate and fear their souls have found release.
Their role in war upon which many frowned
   Has changed in death to peace.

Sleep gently, soldier. Rest your weary head
   Until aroused and ushered to the door,
You find that land, the trumpet call to heed
   Where war shall be no more.

This next poem has been considerably enhanced by the striking use of alliterative key words in every line. This carefully woven repetition of sound adds to the mood and accentuates the message.

THE GLINT OF SUMMER GREEN

Oh, for a scent of summer,
When fields are buntinged brown,
When nature's womb is wizened,
And floribundas frown.

Oh, for the sigh of summer,
Its welcome warmth to know,
When freezing footsteps grumble,
And stumble in the snow.

Oh, to savor summer,
When winter cloisters cold,
When slanted sun fades frosted,
And tired time is old.

Oh, for a sip of summer,
When pewtered is the pond,
When even hearts seem heartless,
Too rigid to respond.

But life is real, rewarding,
Secure, sustained, serene,
When one enrapt, remembers
The glint of summer green.

POETRY PATTERNS
EXPLAINED AND ILLUSTRATED

A BRIEF WORD OF EXPLANATION

Each pattern is first explained and then illustrated with an original poem by the author of the book.

To the left of some poems will appear a rhyme scheme and/or a syllable count. The rhyme scheme is designated with lower case letters, "x" referring to lack of rhyme. Arabic numerals give the syllable count.

For other terminology, refer back to THE POET'S TOOLS.

THE ABERCROMBIE

This form is named after Lascelles Abercrombie (1881–1938); the pattern is taken from his poem "Hymn to Love."* It is written in sets of two stanzas which are linked with each other in an interweaving rhyme scheme. Line 2 of stanza 1 rhymes with line 2 of stanza 2, line 4 of stanza 1 with line 4 of stanza 2. Within each stanza, lines 1 and 3 are rhyme mates. The fourth lines have feminine endings. Lines 1 and 3 are written in pentameter, line 2 in tetrameter, and line 4 in trimeter.

DEVOURED BY A LION

a   Most powerful is the snare set coyly by
b   The first who tried to challenge God,
a   Deceives with clever guile and tempting lie
c   The innocent to falling.

d   Deft master of his craft, he charms and glowers,
b   Chicanery his most used prod.
d   Boldly as a lion he devours,
c   While as a lamb is calling.

e   His plan is simple in efficiency,
f   Unfailing in its sure appeal,
e   Flattering the pride in you and me,
g   Our grasping ego feeding.

h   Ourselves our idol thus, poor Adam's son
f   Breathes on, too blind to see or feel,
h   Unaware of joy we could have won,
g   Unknowing and unheeding.

ACROSTIC

This form might be labelled a poetic oddity in that the meaning is contained in the word formed by reading downward the initial letters of each line.** This characteristic can lead to a wide variety of interesting effects. In the following rhyming example the word spelled out in the beginning letters of the lines is also the title and the theme.

*The original poem is found in the anthology edited by Sir Arthur Quiller–Couch, *The Oxford Book of English Verse* (New York: Oxford University Press, 1941), p. 1124.
**Preminger, p. 4.

INFINITY

I nto the future time stretches its arms,
N ewborn each moment by omniscient schemes,
F resh as the dew over meadows and farms,
I nfused are the fires of passions and dreams.
N ight follows day in the pattern of time,
I nfinite hours wait over the ridge,
T aking their turn in eternity's climb.
Y esterday's gone, and today is the bridge.

The same characteristics are applied in an unrhymed form. In this example alliteration is used; that is, words in the same line begin with the same letter.

ESSENCE

E arnest edicts,
S pirited sincerity
S ignificant similes,
E xpressive excellence,
N otable nuggets,
C aptured conclusions,
E ach is essence.

ADAGEM

An interesting variation of the acrostic, this form and term were originated by Marie L. Blanche Adams. The first words of the lines when read downwards convey a special message.

LIFT UP YOUR EYES

LIFT me up that I might see
UP to where the eagles fly,
YOUR wondrous heights where winds blow free,
EYES unafraid to scan the sky.
UNTO the mountains will I flee,
THE highest point that I might know;
HILLS speak of majesty to me.

AFFLATUS

Webster defines "afflatus" as an "act of blowing or breathing on" and also as an "overmastering impulse."* Applied to poetry, it could mean the influence which inspires a writer to creativity as a direct result of studying the works of another, captivated by the other's mood, message, or philosophy. This example was written after study of "The Legend of Sleepy Hollow" by Washington Irving. The application of this term to poetry is introduced by Viola Berg.

ANOTHER RIDER IN THE HOLLOW

Once upon the shores of Hudson
On the ancient Tappan Zee,
Dozed a sleepy little valley
Pillowed by tranquility.

This quaint neighborhood admitted
To a superstitious blight,
For strange music and queer noises
Haunted travelers in the night.

Eerie chief of midnight orgies,
Headless Hessian trooper's ghost
Rode a black steed in the moonlight
Heading for the graveyard post.

Sober minds gave vent to dreaming
When deep shadows crossed their trail.
Hoofbeats of this spectred stallion
Turned the bravest traveler pale.

Many yarns were told and savored
Polished with a mystic flare
Of the mournful cries and wailings
Heard upon the raven air.

Poor dead Ichabod, abrooding,
Had no chance to ride away.
Dark the night, his soul still darker,
Gripped his mind with strange dismay.

---

*Webster's New International Dictionary, 3rd ed., s.v. "afflatus."

Dire and ghostly were the landmarks,
Ich rode whistling through the glen,
His poor heart grown sore with thumping.
Would the Hessian ride again?

On he rode, with nerves ajangle,
Past poor Andre's tulip tree,
Landed on a bramble thicket,
Petrified as he could be.

There before him edged by moonbeams,
Huge, misshapen, weird and black,
Bounded in his path a monster,
Nightmare cloaked demoniac.

Off rode Ichabod in terror
Clinging to his horse's mane,
Followed by the apparition,
Real it was, but not humane.

Rising in his ghostly stirrups
His pursuer hurled his head.
Ichabod was tumbled headlong
While the dreaded villain fled.

By the dawn our victim vanished.
Rival Bones just wasn't kind,
For we know it was a pumpkin
Made Ich leave his love behind.

Far away in Sleepy Hollow
Rides a ghost who can't forget.
Hear his thumping heart still pounding,
Riding, riding, riding — yet.

For other examples of the AFFLATUS form, see the HERRICK and the FLETCHER.

ALBA

According to Webster, an Alba is a "... love lyric usually dealing with the parting of lovers at dawn."* Written expressly to extol the sunrise, it is the counterpart to the serenade, an evening song.**

*Webster's New International, s.v. "alba."
**Untermeyer, Pursuit, p. 144.

HAIL TO THE SUN

Hail to thee, oh, kingly Sol,
Upon your timely rising.
The dawn has surely come to all,
Of that there's no surmising.
The birds have hailed your coming, sir,
They've prefaced you for hours,
And soon the sleeping buds that were
Will blossom into flowers.

ALEXANDRINE

As a pattern the Alexandrine must be distinguished from the twelve–syllable line also called an Alexandrine, so-called because it was popularized in the 12th century poem "Le Roman d'Alexandre."* (For the use of an **Alexandrine line**, see SPENSE-RIAN STANZA.)

This form contains three Cinquains in iambic meter. (See CIN-QUAIN.) The syllable count for each Cinquain is 2–4–6–8–2; the rhyme scheme is designated at the left.

AN HOUR IN MY HAND

a	Today
b	the hours peal,
a	in turn, for me to pay
a	each one attention, to survey,
b	to feel,
c	to touch
d	and understand
c	how precious and how much
d	an hour is worth within my hand;
c	to clutch
e	it tight
f	and use it well,
f	this passing breath, to dwell
e	within its arms, then bid its light
f	farewell.

*Webster's New International, s.v. "alexandrine."

AMARANTH

Originated by Viola Gardner, this unique form makes deliberate use of the nine most common poetry feet.* To produce something resembling poetry within such rigid limitations is a real test of a writer's command of meter, and if the form is followed correctly, a perfectly balanced piece of writing will be the result. (See METER for an explanation of the less usual metric feet.)

REVEILLE

Spondee	Rise up,
Iamb	to joy
Pyrrhic	of the
Dactyl	wakening
Trochee	morning,
Amphimacer	look and see
Choriamb	light in the east
Anapest	as it sparks
Amphibrach	the heartbeat.

AMPHION

This ten–line poem combines four lines written in tetrameter with three sets of couplets written in dimeter.

I BELIEVE

a	The proof of God is everywhere,
b	Butterflies,
b	Starry skies,
a	The magic in the April air,
c	Joy of spring,
c	Birds that sing,
d	Our love to give and to receive,
e	Sunset glow,
e	Crops that grow;
d	These miracles make me believe.

---

*Jean Calkins, ed. Reprinted from *Handbook on Haiku and Other Form Poems*, by permission of the publisher of J & C Transcripts, copyright © 1970, p. 31.

ANALOGUE

Originated by Rena Ferguson Parks, the Analogue consists of a nine–line stanza written in iambic pentameter. It uses three rhymes, ending with a couplet.

THE OVERFLOW

a	An artist died, and people hardly knew
b	The soul at all, but since he'd gone, aware —
b	That little man, you know, his house all bare
a	Except one room where sunlight blazoned through.
a	But now, quite startled by a first-hand view
b	His neighbors, overcome, could only stare —
b	His gorgeous oils were auctioned everywhere.
c	A shame, you say, he lived in want and dearth?
c	He did not mind. How much is beauty worth?

APOSTROPHE

Untermeyer says that "a poetic apostrophe is a turning to and addressing an absent person as though he were present, an object as though it were a person, an inanimate thing as though it were alive."* When used poetically, this device is a pathway for communication from the human mind to nature and to the inanimate.

SPEAK TO ME, OH, GENTLE WATERS

Speak to me, oh, gentle waters,
Lapping gently at my feet.
Impart to me a precious measure
Of the peace with which you greet
A restless world of people who
Know how to rest no more,
Until they sense what they have missed
When musing on your shore.

A satirical use of apostrophe, originated by Stanley H. Barkan, is a verse form rhymed a–a–x–a. "The name of the person apostrophized provides the determining 'a' rhyme."**

It is certain, Thomas Paine,
Though in rebeldom you reign,
Fire like yours would be tame stuff
In a modern day campaign.

*Untermeyer, *Pursuit*, p. 152.
**Calkins, *Handbook*, p. 29.

ARABESQUE

Created by Lucille Evans, this version features head rhyme in couplets. It has feminine and masculine alternating end words, though no end rhyme is required.* Each line in this example starts with a trochee.

ODE TO WILLIAM SHAKESPEARE

Bringing his sonnets of love everlasting,
Singing his art for us all to enjoy,
Gracing the literate world with emotion,
Lacing his words with such polish and flare;
Weaving his passions, we thrill as we ponder,
Leaving reality, lost in his spell,
Meeting this romeo, feeling his fire,
Greeting the muse, and his powerful pen.
Giving his genius and verses in tribute,
Living for love and the creature so fair,
Heeding this bard is a feeling to treasure
Reading his sonnets we thrill once again.

ARKAHAM BALLAD

This form was originated by Queena Davison Miller. Its unique feature is that the last line of each stanza becomes the first three feet of the next stanza. Minor changes may occasionally appear in the wording. It may contain any number of stanzas. It is composed in iambic meter. Lines 1, 3, and 4 are in tetrameter, lines 2 and 5 in trimeter. The rhyming is x–a–b–b–a. The form is suitable for current events and newspaper headlines. I have stretched this suggestion to include dreams.

THE WAY OF DREAMS

x   Arriving in sub-conscious mists,
a   I do not know from where,
b   A haunting stranger came my way
b   And brought a scent of rose bouquet;
a   I longed to touch her hair.

*Reprinted from *Jean's Journal* (Spring, 1969), p. 38, ed. Jean Calkins, by permission of the publisher of J & C Transcripts, copyright © 1969.

67

x   I longed to touch her hair, and hoped
a   That she would understand.
b   I struggled in my dream, and then
b   From where her lovely hair had been
a   A rose fell in my hand.

THE ARNOLD

This form, named after the poet Matthew Arnold (1822–1888), is patterned after a portion of Arnold's poem, "Hymn of Empedocles."* It is characterized by its five–line stanzas, the first four lines of which are composed in trimeter with alternate rhyming. Every fifth line of all stanzas is written in hexameter, and line 5 of stanza 1 rhymes with line 5 of stanza 2; line 5 of stanza 3 rhymes with line 5 of stanza 4, etc. The fifth line is centered under the previous four.

MORNING STAR OF DAY

a   When restless are the years,
b   And friendless are my days,
a   When efforts end in tears,
b   And hollow is man's praise,
c   How longs my weary soul for purity, for sun.

d   As panteth yet the hart,
e   For waters flowing sweet,
d   As budding gentians part,
e   The sun's rays to entreat,
c   So cleave I unto Thee, oh, matchless Holy One.

f   When downcast is my soul,
g   The path ahead so steep,
f   When crashing billows roll,
g   And troubled is my sleep,
h   I ache and yearn, my God, Thy countenance to see.

i   Oh, hear me when I pray,
j   I seek Thy loving face,
i   Thou Morning Star of day,
j   Thy wisdom to embrace,
h   I hunger and I thirst, to eat and drink of Thee.

*Quiller-Couch, pp. 923-24.

BACCRESEIZE (Bŏck–cre–sēizé)

This beautiful twelve–line form was originated by E. Ernest Murrell. It uses eight and four syllable line refrains. The short line occurs in lines 4, 8, and 12. Line 1 repeats as line 7, and its last four syllables are repeated as the last part of line 2.

JANUARY BLIZZARD

A	The winter storm, the winter storm,
a	The fury of the winter storm
x	Descends upon a helpless world
B	With swirling snow,
b	Relentless winds with swirling snow.
x	Resignedly the earth accepts
A	The winter storm, the winter storm
B	With swirling snow.
x	But snugly by the fireside
x	I watch the avalanche descend,
x	So glad the wind must stay outside
B	With swirling snow.

BALANCE

The beauty of this interesting form is in its ebb and flow of thought. The twenty lines are balanced by the syllable count as designated and by the rhyme scheme. Following the ebb and flow, all ten–syllable lines rhyme, as do the eight–syllable lines, the sixes, fours, and twos. The first line is repeated in the last line.* Smoothness is needed for balance and beauty.

WHERE ROSES BLOOMED

10	A	A little house was waiting in the shade.
8	b	Most people passed by on the road
6	c	beyond the battered fence,
4	d	and didn't see
2	e	a thing.
2	e	But spring,
4	d	so bold and free,
6	c	with utmost confidence
8	b	implanted seeds and wild flowers sowed,

*Calkins, *Handbook*, p. 32.

10	a	and shared its magic touch, all undismayed,
10	a	around the sorry shack where time had strayed,
8	b	and blessed the broken-down abode
6	c	with pink magnificence,
4	d	its pageantry
2	e	to bring.
2	e	Oh, fling
4	d	your harmony
6	c	with song-thrush elegance;
8	b	the roses joined in joyous ode.
10	A	A little house was waiting in the shade.

BALLAD

The ballad is a short story, expressed in rhythm and rhyme, which had its origin from the people and has become a folk-song. Its action was usually swift, and its language was simple. The ballad-makers paraphrased legends and gave them the aura of myths, translating the news of the times, including feuds, tragedies, murders, exploits, and star-crossed loves.*

Many changes have come about since the ancient times of the first ballad-makers. Communication has been taken over by the motion pictures, the television networks, the daily paper, and the paperback. Yet ballads still persist. During the early development of our country, the pioneers and early settlers localized the ancient tales and added their own new incidents and flavor. Folklore has always been kept alive in country and western music. Most ballads use a refrain line as a kind of chorus.

BALLAD OF THE BEDOUINS

There once was a father, El-Farid, his name,
  Who lived far beyond the Red Sea,
And he had a daughter, a sweet little daughter,
  And a bright little gypsy was she.
They lived in the desert, the great lonely desert,
  Where not many nomads passed through
To see that his daughter, his now-grown up daughter
  Had a face that was ugly to view.
    Oh, play the lute sweetly, give ear to my song,
    And blow, desert breezes, my story along.

---

*Untermeyer, *Pursuit*, p. 153-54.

He loved his shy Zara, his sweet ugly Zara,
  And so he resolved for her sake
That no one should ever remove her kind veil,
  And no one her soft heart would break.
For she had a beauty of spirit and mind
   So her unsightly face he could bear,
But I know the men of this desert, thought he.
   They desire a woman more fair.
     Oh, play the lute sweetly, give ear to my song,
     And blow, desert breezes, my story along.

So he told his sweet daughter, "Oh, Zara, my love,
  I desire a promise of thee,
That you'll never depart from the tent of your kin,
  I want you forever with me."
That night on her pillow her thoughts wandered far
  For a spirit so docile and meek,
For on that same morning, just hours before
  She had seen the dark eyes of a sheik.
     Oh, play the lute sweetly, give ear to my song,
     And blow, desert breezes, my story along.

She knew he had noticed her graceful young form
  As she danced on the sands in the dawn,
For he had appeared on the brow of the dune,
  ...Took a bold look, and was gone.
She dreamed of this gypsy, but deeply she cared
  For her father who loved her so true.
Her soul was quite torn for she felt HE'd return,
  And her heart told her what she would do.
     Oh, play the lute sweetly, give ear to my song,
     And blow, desert breezes, my story along.

In the full of the moon Abu rode from the east
  And spirited Zara away.
Her heart beat so wildly and shuddered with joy
  On this longed-for Jamilian* day.
Over the Jordan and Yemen they flew
  To the tents of the gypsies in Kaid,
And on that same night he removed her black veil
  And gazed on the face of the maid.
     Oh, play the lute sweetly, give ear to my song,
     And blow, desert breezes, my story along.

*Jamil was the creator of Arabian love poetry.

His visage so flushed with excitement and hope
   And his lips which were ready to kiss
Changed in a moment; he thought to himself,
   I can't love a maiden like this.
So firmly he drew the veil over her eyes,
   And quickly they mounted his steed,
And all the deep vales and the dunes they retraced
   With determined and thundering speed.
     Oh, play the lute sweetly, give ear to my song,
     And blow, desert breezes, my story along.

Poor Zara crept in to the tent of her kin
   Rejected, unwanted, and spurned.
In Abu's shocked eyes she had seen the harsh truth
   And the facts of her face she had learned.
Hopes and fond dreams were replaced by despair.
   With awakening tears, Zara cried,
And now she could see that her father's kind love
   Was for her sweet spirit inside.
     Oh, play the lute sweetly, give ear to my song,
     And blow, desert breezes, my story along.

Never again would she leave her home tent;
   No swain would seek after her hand.
Her veil was her comfort and only in dreams
   Would her spirit fly over the sand.
She chants her sad song on her lute of four strings
   In dulcet tones, whispered and low,
Of a maiden grown old in a Bedouin tent
   And a love which she never would know.
     Oh, play the lute sweetly, give ear to my song,
     And blow, desert breezes, my story along.

BALLAD STANZA (See QUATRAIN.)

BALLADE

Described by Webster, the Ballade is one of the more elaborate French forms. Its intricate structure gives it an air of sophistication, tempting only the most ambitious. This strict form was established in the Middle Ages by French poets* who patterned its three stanzas of eight lines and an envoy of four lines. The last line of each stanza is an identical refrain which is the cornerstone of the Ballade. The **envoy** is a summing up of the poem and is used as a dedication of the lines. The rhymes as well as the arrangement are the same in all stanzas, and no rhyme word or syllable may be repeated. The strict rhyme scheme is designated at the left for the stanzas and the envoy.

THE FACES OF RESPECT

a	Through these strangely tense and anxious years
b	Our countrymen have heard the hue and cry
a	Of underprivileged groups, whose hopes and fears
b	Have grown to such proportions to supply
b	The headlines in our news, to terrify
c	The law abiding public, to deflect
b	The mainstream of our thoughts. Can we deny
C	The time has come for all to learn respect?
a	Whatever so-called perfect plan appears
b	Our Government just cannot be drained dry
a	By welfare handouts just to hear the cheers
b	Of rioters whose dreams have proved a lie
b	Infringing on the innocent whereby
c	Contemptuousness has sparked the most select
b	And caused long hoped-for goals to go awry.
C	The time has come for all to learn respect.
a	The law which every thinking man reveres
b	Must be upheld that truth might fill our sky,
a	Our courts, our schools, and modern cavaliers
b	Must take their place with strength to prophesy,
b	Defend the masses; none should question why,
c	The tide of truth once more to flow unchecked,
b	To infiltrate our law which must not die.
C	The time has come for all to learn respect.

*Untermeyer, *Pursuit*, p. 160.

b	Rebellious trends can be no ruthless pry;
c	Regard for proper law will yet protect
b	The mass of faithful citizens who try.
C	The time has come for all to learn respect.

BALLADE WITH DOUBLE REFRAIN

One of the two refrains "occurs in the middle of each stanza, the other in the usual place at the end of each stanza. Both refrains are repeated in the envoy." As Untermeyer also points out, "the two refrains are usually opposite in nature, presenting either a contradiction in character or a sharp contrast in mood."* This form has a structure of three eight–line stanzas and a four–line envoy, with only three rhyming sounds allowed in the entire poem.

LIFE IS A RHYTHM

a	Through the season's cold we sniffle and sneeze
b	And bear the brunt of the wintering,
a	But the spirit longs for the April breeze
B	And the welcome kiss of the waking spring.
b	We join the thrust of the flurrying
c	To the crowning yield of fruit, and then
b	In the aftermath of harvesting
C	We sigh for the peace of the hearth again.
a	But after a siege of frost and freeze
b	The rhythmed pendulum starts to swing,
a	And the pilgrim seeks for warmth to please
B	And the welcome kiss of the waking spring.
b	The tempo rises with gardening
c	To the heights of demanding regimen.
b	When the holds of the barns are flourishing
C	We sigh for the peace of the hearth again.
a	Once more the tides of time will tease
b	And prompt the soul to purposing,
a	To grasp the metronomed trapeze,
B	And the welcome kiss of the waking spring.
b	With rising force to fly on wing
c	To the sweeping force of summer's ken,
b	Content as our harvest fruit we bring
C	We sigh for the peace of the hearth again.

*Untermeyer, *Pursuit,* p. 167.

b	Man yearns for the time of blossoming,
B	And the welcome kiss of the waking spring
c	Leads to our greatest triumph when
C	We sigh for the peace of the hearth again.

DOUBLE BALLADE

A variant of the Ballade, this form is not to be confused with the Ballade With Double Refrain. In addition to the regular envoy, this has double the usual number of stanzas, each ordinarily consisting of eight lines.* Every verse concludes with the same line, and the rhyming scheme is identical in every verse, using three rhyming sounds only, and not repeating any consonants or consonant clusters if at all possible.

TO SEE THE LIGHT

a	The masses wander down path and lane,
b	Are chilled by the winds that tease and blow,
a	And then are pushed right back again.
b	The skies seem dark and the clouds seem low
b	To the man who is buffeted to and fro,
c	But there is a space where the sky is bright
b	Where the laser beam shows the way to go,
C	But eyes must be raised to see the light.
a	The crowd is aware of the cold and rain,
b	And the rainbow hues of long ago,
a	But their hopeful travels seem in vain
b	When the currents push and pull them so.
b	Who is friend and who is foe?
c	They gaze about in the endless night
b	If only a little warmth to know,
C	But eyes must be raised to see the light.
a	The restless whimper and cry with pain,
b	Baffled by weather and bogged by snow.
a	The journey seems such an awful strain;
b	If only a little gleam would show.
b	They look to the right and the left although
c	Their brothers are caught in the same sad plight.
b	They hope for the warmth of a candle's glow,
C	But eyes must be raised to see the light.

*Untermeyer, *Pursuit*, p. 168.

a   The plodders are bound to the onbound train
b   And the number of journeyers seems to grow,
a   And many are those who wilt and wane,
b   And many a marcher deserts his row.
b   Vanished is braggadocio,
c   For scarce is the strength or will to fight.
b   The simple truth is apropos,
C   But eyes must be raised to see the light.

a   The wanderers bear the mark of Cain
b   As they strive for a spot on this earth below,
a   A place to rest in the rough terrain,
b   And search for cheer in the gray tableau.
b   But there is no halt for those that sow
c   The tares and weeds on their earthly flight,
b   For what they plant they shall also mow,
C   But eyes must be raised to see the light.

a   When will the weary mob obtain
b   Their fill of oratorio?
a   When will the fruit of harvest grain
b   Become the traveller's ultimo?
b   For he must walk and he must row
c   Through the vales and streams to reach the height,
b   Before he can see the portico,
C   But eyes must be raised to see the light.

THE BINYON

This seven-line rhymed form is patterned after the much quoted poem, "O World, Be Nobler," written by Laurence Binyon* (1869–1943). The form begins and ends with the same line, has its own rhyming scheme, and is composed in iambic tetrameter.

INVITATION TO FLY

A   My child, lift up your timid eyes,
b   Clip not your wings before you start,
c   For life is calling everywhere,
c   And rainbows wait for those who dare.
b   Oh, taste and see, shy trembling heart,
a   And gaze into inviting skies.
A   My child, lift up your timid eyes.

*Quiller-Couch, p. 1087.

BLANK VERSE

An unrhymed form, blank verse is usually written in iambic penta-meter, referred to as **heroic blank verse.** Most meditative poetry and nearly all poetic drama have been composed in this medium. Untermeyer observes that because the rhythm of iambic penta-meter is so close to speech, and is therefore so flexible, scholars consider it to be the most important meter in the literature of the western world.* Blank verse is not confined to stanzas of uniform length. The breaks come at the conclusion of thoughts, as para-graphs in prose. The freedom of expression in blank verse lends itself to the use of **run-on lines,** which to complete their meaning, run over to the next line without a pause.

THEY MET THEIR GOD

Through cold and snow they walked to find the house
Of God, then laid their flintlock muskets down,
Removed their hats and shawls, and sat alert
On rough hewn benches, stiff, and straight, and hard.
But there they met their God. No Indian threat
Could keep them home the first day of the week.
Too much they had endured to forego this,
The chance to worship as their conscience taught.

Their preacher in his earthy homespun clothes
Had much to say of courage and of faith,
And led their simple worship of their God,
Who brought them safely to this strange new land.

The sermon over and the last hymn sung,
They cautiously retraced their guarded steps,
This pious band again walked through the snow,
Thus fortified, to face another week.

Though both free verse and blank verse are without end rhyme, blank verse has a regular structure.** The following example was written in trochaic tetrameter, using feminine endings in the first three lines, and a masculine word in the fourth.

*Untermeyer, *Pursuit*, p. 171.
**Untermeyer, *Pursuit*, p. 172.

SOLDIERS ON THE ROOF

Falling, falling are the raindrops
In a frenzied wild profusion,
Like ten-thousand soldiers marching
On the eardrums of my heart.

Faster, faster come the armies,
Overcoming by their numbers,
Tiny boots combine to thunder,
Pounding out a drum tatoo.

Slow, and slower, now a patter,
Last detachment finds the drainpipe,
Breezes clear the scene of battle,
Far away a bugle calls.

THE BLUNDEN

Named after Edmund Blunden (1896–1933), this form was patterned from his beautiful poem, "The Survival."* It features stanzas of six lines each with rhyme scheme. Lines 1, 3, 4, and 5 are written in iambic tetrameter, lines 2 and 6 in iambic trimeter. This combination of rhythms gives this form a satisfying swing.

TO KEEP OUR BROTHER

a   We hear the plaintive voices call,
b   We see the starving die.
c   We feel the ache within their core,
c   Their eager hungering for more.
a   Some have no chance, no hope at all,
b   And vainly search the sky.

d   We listen, yet we have not heard,
e   We see, and yet are blind.
f   The world needs brothers who will care,
f   Samaritans to heal, to share,
d   For love is just a misused word
e   Unless we make it kind.

*Quiller-Couch, p. 1140.

BOUTONNIERE

This patterned poem of thirteen lines which was originated by Ann Byrnes Smith is composed in trochaic tetrameter and is catalectic — lacking one syllable in the final foot, accounting for the seven–syllable lines.* The first two lines of this form are also its last two lines, bringing the message back to its beginning. The rhyme pattern is strict.

LAUGHTER LIVED HERE

A–1	Laughter lived here long ago,
A–2	Why she left I do not know.
b	Trembling voices faintly call,
b	Echoes scale the crumbling wall,
c	Eerily one feels the tears
c	Caught in faded, haunted fears
c	Shackled in these rooms for years,
b	Casting such a somber pall
d	Over threshold, arch, and floor,
d	Closing tight each rusting door;
d	Life and loving are no more.
A–1	Laughter lived here long ago,
A–2	Why she left I do not know.

BRAGI

This form, created by Thelma Allinder, was made popular by the poetry publication, *Scimitar and Song*. It consists of two six–line stanzas with syllable count of 6–8–10–10–8–6 and 10–8–6–6–8–10 respectively, rhyming a–b–c–c–b–a and c–b–a–a–b–c. It is suited especially for scenic beauty and for the elfin.

SUNRISE TO SUNSET

6	a	A sleepy world bestirs
8	b	As eastern skies exude their light,
10	c	And sunbeams dance on meadowland and hill.
10	c	All nature's creatures answer to the thrill,
8	b	The birds and butterflies take flight;
6	a	A kitten wakes and purrs,

*Calkins, *Handbook*, p. 34.

10	c	Until at noon no more of light could fill
8	b	The sultry air. Then at its height
6	a	The world revolves, incurs
6	a	Its greatest strength, prefers
8	b	To slow its tempo toward the night.
10	c	With setting sun once more the world is still.

BREVEE (Brē-vēe)

Created by Marie L. Blanche Adams, this form is one of the shortest in existence, its lines being written entirely in monometer and dimeter. It contains two stanzas of six lines each, with strict rhyming scheme.

KATCHOO!

a	Shorty,
a	Sporty
b	Mini skirts,
c	Teasing,
c	Sneezing
b	Carefree flirts.
d	Daring,
d	Baring
e	Brave and bold,
f	Chilly
f	Millie
e	Caught a cold!

THE BRIDGES

This patterned form, named for Robert Bridges (1844–1930), and taken from his poem, "Nightingales,"* features long and short lines in exact rhyming scheme. The short lines are centered under the longer lines. Lines 1, 2, and 4 of each stanza are composed in iambic hexameter, line 5 in pentameter, and lines 3 and 6 in dimeter.

*Quiller-Couch, p. 1016.

80

WAIT TILL NEXT YEAR!

a So worshipped are the numbered forms before their eyes,
a Displaying razored skills, that swelling spirits rise
b   To new extremes.
c The sun lends festive rays across the diamond green,
c And through the fired-crowds wild thoughts careen
b   With pennant dreams.

d Within their view each Hercules performs in turn,
d Coordinating muscled power, with yen to earn
e   His bit of fame.
f The glories and the agonies, the joys, the blues,
f All run their course within the fan who views
e   A baseball game.

BRIOLETTE (Brī-o-lettĕ)

This new form, introduced by Viola Berg, may contain any number of stanzas, each stanza containing a tercet and a couplet. It is composed in iambic tetrameter.

MARIANNE

a Where magic is awakening,
a Where gypsies dance and laugh and sing,
a Where jonquils bloom with joy of spring,
b Where dreams ignore all curb and ban,
b This Shangrila spells Marianne.

c Where unfenced breezes waft so free,
c Where silver moonbeams kiss the sea,
c Where elves join imps for pixie tea,
d Where hope is born and love is new,
d Without a doubt, she'll be there, too.

e For all of life she wants to taste,
e It's not for storing, not for waste,
e And her own pathways she has traced.
f Where pulsing action geysers free,
f That's where Marianne will be.

THE BRYANT

This form is patterned after the poem, "To A Waterfowl" by William Cullen Bryant* (1794–1878). It is constructed in four–line stanzas with alternate rhyming. Lines 1 and 4 are in trimeter, lines 2 and 3 in pentameter. The short lines are indented.

TO SOAR ALOFT

a   Shackled, I limp my way
b   Enchained to earthbound tasks which must be done.
a   I cannot thrive, so censored is my day
b   Without the warmth of sun.

c   Must I through life remain
d   Destined to a sphere of hampered tongue?
c   The songs, unborn, haunt me to fade again,
d   Receding and unsung.

e   Surely inside of me
f   Within the soul where I have ventured oft
e   I'll find an unfenced freer galaxy
f   In which to soar aloft.

BURNS STANZA (See SESTET.)

CADENCE**

This seven–line free verse form originated with Ella M. Cunningham. The twenty–seven syllables are arranged 1–2–3–4–4–8–5. The first word in line 1 and the last word of every line should be a strong word (not an article or preposition).

YOUR MORNING DREAMS

1   Sleep,
2   my child.
3   The dawn greets
4   the sleepy sky
4   with gentle kiss,
8   tenderly caressing with love
5   your innocent dreams.

*The work is found in the anthology edited by Curtis Hadden Page, *The Chief American Poets* (New York: Houghton, Mifflin & Co., 1905), pp. 3, 4.
**CADENCE (For use as a poetic device, see ADDITIONAL TOOLS.)

CAMEO

Originated by Alice Maud Spokes,* the Cameo is a free verse form containing seven lines with exact syllable count. Each line must end on a strong word.

ANGEL SONG

2	Music
5	ecstatic, joyful,
8	played upon a mighty organ,
3	harmony
8	like a choir of cherubim
7	echoing a celestial
2	amen.

CANOPUS

This form differs slightly in its rhyming arrangement from the Sonnette (see SONNETTE) in that its pattern is a–b–a–b–c–b–c. It is similar in its seven lines of iambic pentameter and in the continuous flow of its thought.**

MONARCH OF THE NIGHT

a	Our nation's birthday is a time for fun,
b	When fireworks light up the heavenly stage.
a	Bold shooting stars sent skyward from a gun,
b	And neon geysers bolted from their cage
c	Perform an act of brilliance and of noise,
b	The moon beams down, observing as a sage,
c	And mutely smiles at man's pathetic toys.

CARYOTTE

This twelve–line form was originated by Robert Cary.*** It is composed in dactylic dimeter with one syllable lacking in the second foot. Each couplet has both head and tail rhyme.

---

*Calkins, *Handbook*, p. 35.
**From *The Complete Rhyming Dictionary and Poet's Craft Book* by Clement Wood. Copyright 1936 by Gloria Goddard Wood. Reprinted by permission of Doubleday & Company, Inc.
***Jean Calkins, ed., *Jean's Journal* (June–July, 1971), p. 15.

PARADE OF THE HOURS

a–b	Sweet and anointed,
a–b	Fleet and appointed,
c–d	Hale and respected,
c–d	Frail and connected,
e–f	Sure and proceeding,
e–f	Pure in its leading,
g–h	Nude in its showing,
g–h	Viewed and then flowing,
i–j	Tall years of plodding,
i–j	Small minutes prodding,
k–l	Prime in direction,
k–l	Time is perfection.

CAVATINA

This form by Hannah Kahn alternates five feet and two feet lines, concluding with a couplet in pentameter. Line 2 rhymes with line 4, line 6 with line 8. The mood should be reflective, leading up to a strong climax. The Cavatina has some of the characteristics of the LuVailean Sonnet.

BEYOND THE BEATEN PATH

Away from push and prod and constant din
    I flee away,
Far beyond the beaten path to seek
    A calmer day,
As from the heart of nature I absorb
    A healing balm,
And join my spirit with its song and rest,
    Serene and calm.
My thirst is quenched by mystic wine, and then
I rise refreshed to face the world again.

CHAIN LANTERNE (See LANTERNE.)

CHAIN VERSE

Wood defines chain verse as "any repetition of a rhyme, word, phrase, line or group of lines, to tie up a section of the poem with the succeeding section."* In this example the lines are intertwined, the second line of the first verse used as the first line of the next verse. This sequence is carried on through the poem, ending with the first line. The rhyming scheme also intertwines.

ANOTHER DAY UNFOLDS

a   Another day unfolds before my eyes,
b   The hours, precise and silent, filter through,
a   Each one for me a challenge and a prize,
b   Each one a virgin in its mute debut.

b   The hours, precise and silent, filter through,
c   As years of days roll gently down the hill,
b   Each minute has its place in special view,
c   And then departs and is forever still.

c   As years of days roll gently down the hill,
d   Their tempo seems to mount. It is not so.
c   Each hour its sixty minutes will fulfill,
d   But not a second more will overflow.

d   Their tempo seems to mount. It is not so.
a   Each hour just seems more precious as it flies.
d   Then lost forever in the sunset glow,
a   Another day unfolds before my eyes.

CHANT ROYAL

Untermeyer points out that the Chant Royal, a larger form of the Ballade, is one of the rarer French forms. It is so called because it was supposed to be sung before kings.** It consists of five stanzas of eleven lines and an envoy which follows the rhyming pattern of the previous lines. The difficulty in structuring a Chant Royal is in the confinement to only five rhyming sounds. Also, it requires a subject large enough so that the writer can keep building his theme, which is to be tied neatly together in the envoy. No rhyme words may be used twice except in the envoy.

*Wood, p. 74.
**Untermeyer, *Pursuit*, p. 178. See also Preminger, p. 115.

THE GOD WHO CANNOT DIE

a	Some voices raised in doubt say God is dead,
b	For since they cannot see Him, then they claim
a	That He in all His magnitude had fled
b	Away from planet Earth, and that His name
c	No longer means a thing; He does not care,
c	(If He is still alive), and even prayer
d	Is wasted now. They say He does not show
d	His power to man, the wrongs to overthrow.
e	As pessimistic as the Pharisee
d	They shake their wagging heads in doom and woe.
E	God is alive, and evermore shall be!

a	"Oh, Man, you say I died? Such lies you spread
b	About the God who is? To your own shame
a	You've slandered Me; your empty tales have fed
b	To those who listened to your silly game.
c	Oh, little man, the heavens all declare
c	My glory. Can you turn aside, despair?
d	The moon and stars still orbit to and fro,
d	And life still thrives in mass and embryo.
e	Oh, stumbling man, look from yourselves to Me.
d	Where would the Rock of All the Ages go?"
E	God is alive, and evermore shall be!

a	"I sent My Son; for you He suffered, bled,
b	And took upon Himself the sinners' blame,
a	And every kingly right He forfeited;
b	To be lost Adam's sacrifice, His aim.
c	Are you so bound within the devil's lair
c	You do not see Christ suffered for you there?
d	He gave His life; He died that man might know
d	My life anew which evermore would flow
e	To those who look in faith to Calvary,
d	Rejoicing that the grave is not their foe."
E	God is alive and evermore shall be!

a	"Poor misled man, so wrong in what you said,
b	So weak and starved the spirit in your frame,
a	You do not see that life is in the Bread,
b	And death has died because to earth Christ came.
c	How sad to fall into the devil's snare,
c	To let him blind you, keep you unaware
d	Of truth which lives, My spirit all aglow —

d   Christ's resurrection shook the world below.
e   We share Our life in answer to man's plea,
d   Love, grace, and peace, My presence shall bestow."
E   God is alive, and evermore shall be!

a   "For through My Comforter my light is shed,
b   The mortal spirit fueled by My flame;
a   Man's fear removed when by My Spirit led,
b   Earth cannot curb nor heaven's power tame.
c   You do not need to see Me to compare
c   The joys of fellowship, My child, My heir,
d   For you the cleansing fountain flows although
d   The unbelieving have not found it so.
e   For those who search in faith My face to see
d   I'm real enough; to Me their breath they owe."
E   God is alive, and evermore shall be!

d   "Oh, Universe, My Spirit is aglow;
d   Where heart doors open, there I gladly go
e   To indwell now, and for eternity.
d   Open your eyes, that you might see and know
E   God is alive, and evermore shall be!"

CHILDREN'S POETRY (See OCCASIONAL POETRY.)

CINQUAIN

A five–line unrhymed stanza, its name is derived from the French word *cinque*, meaning five. This form, invented by Adelaide Crapsey, is reminiscent of the Japanese Tanka.* The syllable count is given. The strong word ending each line gives the Cinquain its balance and dignity. Its form is ideal for reflective thought.

THE BREAD OF LIFE

2   Jesus
4   fed five thousand
6   on the grassy hillside,
8   and there was enough left over
2   for me.

*Untermeyer, *Pursuit*, p. 181. See also Calkins, *Handbook*, p. 35.

DOUBLE CINQUAIN

A development from the Cinquain, this form contains ten un-rhymed lines, each line ending on a strong word, giving balance, strength, and grace to the poem.

SPELLBOUND

2	My star
2	teases
4	and enchants me,
4	gleaming up there,
6	daring me to notice
6	its exploding fire,
8	igniting my soul with the joy
8	of its mysterious twinkle.
2	With awe
2	I stare.

RHYMED CINQUAIN

Shelley made use of the following form of the Cinquain through-out his poem "To a Skylark."* The first four lines have three poe-tic feet, and the last line has six. Shelley indented the second and fourth lines, and centered the last line under the first four.

JOURNEY OF THE SOUL

a	Reason quite forsook me,
b	My poor heart was stirred,
a	My experience shook me
b	With thoughts I'd never heard,
b	Visions are too mystic for language or for word.

CINQUETUN

The rhyme scheme of this form originated by E. Ernest Murrell differentiates it from most of the short poems. Line 1 rhymes with line 4; line 3 with 6; lines 2 and 5 are unrhymed. The syllable count is 8–6–10–6–8–2.**

*Wood, p. 44.
**Calkins, *Handbook*, p. 36.

NIGHT IN FAIRYLAND
(View of New York from a Helicopter)

8	a	Giant blue and white bird lifts its
6	x	eager revolving wings
10	b	into the magic panoramic glow
6	a	of the city, and flits
8	x	over Lilliputian playground
2	b	below.

CINQUINO

This free verse sentence form, invented by James Neille Northe, reverses the syllable count of the three middle lines of the Cinquain, making the syllable count 2–8–6–4–2.

ALONE

Twilight
crouches in undefined sadness;
even the shadows know
that I do not
belong.

CIRCLET

Designed by Rena Ferguson Parks, this ten–line poem is typed or printed double spaced to form a circle. Its rhyme scheme and syllable count are as follows: A–b–c–d–e; e–d–c–b–A and 2–4–6–8–10; 10–8–6–4–2. The Circlet is akin to the Medallion.

LOVE

That word
creates some doubt
because of overuse,
we hardly know the meaning now,
and seek a synonym to take its place.
Is there another filled with kindly grace
which says the same, expressing how
I feel, so you'll deduce
my heart without
that word?

CLERIHEW

The inventor of this verse form is author Edmund Clerihew Bentley. In the two couplets, one line — usually the first — names a famous person, and the other lines treat of characteristics of his personality or an episode — most likely fictitious — of his career.* Truth and seriousness are not necessary characteristics. A light touch provides the best climate for a successful Clerihew.

> Poet Edgar Allan Poe
> Wrote of ghosts who didn't show,
> Chained them all in lair and haven,
> Gave the latch-key to a raven.

COMMEMORATIVE VERSE (See OCCASIONAL POETRY.)

COMPLETE COUPLET (See COUPLET.)

COMPLETE QUATRAIN (See QUATRAIN.)

COMPOSITE SONNET (See SONNET.)

COUPLET

Couplets are paired rhymes in immediate succession. In the 18th century the couplet was developed to its greatest perfection by Alexander Pope.** Since the beginnings of poetry, the couplet has been used extensively; it infiltrates our western literature.

COMPLETE COUPLET

A couplet is referred to as "complete" if it expresses a complete thought within itself.

> In this war-scarred world of care
> Peace can still be found through prayer.

UNEVEN COUPLET

Most couplets are even in length, but couplets may also be composed of paired lines of different lengths.***

---

*Untermeyer, *Pursuit*, p. 182.
** Untermeyer, *Pursuit*, p. 186. See also Calkins, *Handbook*, p. 36.
***Untermeyer, p. 187.

INVITING LULLABY

Beyond the limits of my sight
In fancy's flight
I hear the singing in my dream
Of magic stream,
Teasing when I'm busiest
To come and rest,
Soothing with its lullaby,
Such as I.

HEROIC COUPLET

Written in heroic meter — iambic pentameter — the lines are usually end-stopped, coming to a logical pause.*

If mankind profits from mistakes of yore,
We know a better future is in store.

OPEN COUPLET

Some poets have used enjambment**(e.g. Donne) freely in their heroic couplet compositions, a second line being needed to complete the thought.

The acts of man cannot be judged apart
From all the feelings welling in the heart.

OCTOSYLLABIC COUPLETS

Written in iambic or trochaic tetrameter,*** this form has eight syllables to the line. The following example makes use of both the open and closed couplet pairs.

BALLAD BISCUITS

She dreams of poems through the day,
And thinks of rhythm, rhyme, and sway,
Arranging syllables and such,
And giving verse her special touch.
I hope she finds the kitchen right,
I'm bringing home my appetite.
She'll start the meal with chewy verbs,
Choose adjectives for tasty herbs,

*Untermeyer, *Pursuit*, p. 206.
** See ADDITIONAL TOOLS.
***Preminger, p. 156.

Some limericks added just for spice,
A sonnet casserole is nice,
Some ballad biscuits baked real well,
And for dessert a villanelle.
I'm skin and bones, but she can't see
That I can't live on poetry.
Poetic phrases for the soul
Provide at meals a meager dole.
So, please, dear Muse, for mercy's sake,
I'm waiting for a T-bone steak.

CROMORNA

This three–stanza form is exacting in its structure and challenging in its compactness. The six three–syllable lines rhyme with each other.

BOSTON, 1775

5	a	Farmers were ready,
3	b	Steeled of will,
5	a	Their muskets steady,
3	b	Boding ill.
5	c	Red Coats invading,
3	b	Primed to kill,
5	c	Brisk cannonading,
3	b	Screaming, shrill.
5	d	Rebels' desire
3	b	To fulfill;
5	d	Hot was the fire,
3	b	Red, the hill.

CROSS LIMERICK (See LIMERICK.)

CYCLE

This three–stanza form, especially suited for the mystical, the supernatural, the reflective, was created by Paul Emile Miller. It exhibits both an unusual rhyme scheme and a lovely rhythm. The rhyme in the second and fourth lines of every stanza is the same. Within each stanza, lines 1 and 3 rhyme and have feminine endings. The first and third lines contain a dactyl and three trochees; the second and fourth contain three iambs.

UNSHACKLED

a	There in the flames before me burning,
b	I heard the final sigh;
a	Gone is the blaze of youthful yearning,
b	The dreams of years gone by.
c	Zeal, now eclipsed by heat of fire,
b	Consumed without a cry;
c	Seared are the haunting notes so dire,
b	The songs I would not try.
d	Burn, let them burn, in my memory fading,
b	For now, unchained am I;
d	Freed in the flame, the chaff cascading,
b	Oh, let the ashes fly!

THE CYCLUS

The peculiar interest of this twelve–line iambic form is created by the cycling syllable count, the repetition of line 6 in line 12, and the rhyming of lines 3 and 9. The pattern was created by Marvin Davis Winsett.

WITH GIANT HAND

2	The sun
4	slowly invades
6	the gray darkness with gleams,
6	and stirs to wakening
4	the dreamer from
2	his dreams,
2	beaming
4	the call to rise
6	and to follow his schemes,
6	parting with giant hand
4	the dreamer from
2	his dreams.

DECANNELLE

The pattern for this ten–line stanza created by Joseph N. Nutter was made popular in California in 1949 *Chromotonea*. It is composed in trochaic tetrameter, and every other line is without rhyme. Because of the required syllable count, the odd-numbered lines end with feminine words.

ABANDONED

8	x	Deep within a hidden valley
7	a	Waits a little church in tears,
8	x	Left alone with only memories,
7	a	Keeping vigil through the years.
8	x	Once strong frame and roof now warping,
7	a	Cruel weather feeds its fears.
8	x	Broken pews are mute, forsaken,
7	b	Windows blink in sunset glow.
8	x	Grieving lonely little chapel,
7	b	Did God really have to go?

DECATHLON

This ten–line stanza devised by Anne Pendleton is composed in iambic meter. The syllable count and rhyme scheme are given. This form is suited to the fervid, the triumphant, and the fantastic, and to land and seascapes.

A CUP OF WATER

8	a	Our Father sees a soul in need
8	x	And reaches down to soothe and heal.
4	b	His arm can span
8	x	The weary miles, His tender heart
4	a	Can intercede
8	c	And lift from sorrow and despair
8	c	And give a cloak of strength to wear.
4	b	But in His plan
10	d	He uses human tools in His design.
10	d	Oh, may the hand you use, oh, God, be mine.

THE DE LA MARE

This form is named for Walter De La Mare (1873–1956), and is patterned after his poem "Fare Well."* Effective in its use of long and short lines — three tetrameter followed by dimeter — this pattern alternates feminine and masculine word endings. Only the masculine requires rhyme.

BOOMERANG

With choice bits of idle chatter
Thinking nothing of the cost
Near and far I threw life's pebbles,
Carelessly tossed.
Each harsh word pierced as an arrow,
Bruising deeply, and you cried.
While your spirit did the bleeding,
My spirit died.

THE DE TABLEY

Named for John Leicester Warren, Lord De Tabley (1835–1895), this pattern is from his poem, "Chorus from 'Medea.'"** This form also varies line lengths, alternating iambic pentameter and trimeter. The resulting pleasing balance is enhanced by rhyming alternating lines.

HEADSTONE FOR THE OLD WEST

Nostalgic hearts still ride the cactus trail
From out the fenceless past.
Old timers reminisce a tender tale
From storehouse wild and vast.

On Wild West days the boots come out for show,
The lonely wind still shrieks,
And women blossom forth in calico
To show their best antiques.

The genuine is shrinking every year
As eastward skytrails burn,
Escorting to the cities far and near
The folk who don't return.

*Quiller-Couch, pp. 1108-09.
**Quiller-Couch, p. 977.

DICKSEE (See FRIEZE.)

DICKSON NOCTURNE

This twelve–line form was originated by Margaret Ball Dickson, formerly head of Creative Writing at Valparaiso University, Indiana. Eight lines are in dactylic dimeter and four are catalectic (lacking some syllables in the last dactyl).* Lines 3, 7, and 12 are the same. This repeated line, which serves as a refrain, must fit in smoothly with the message of the poem.

BUT I MUST TRY

a	Thunder and rainclouds meet,
a	Aiming to halt my feet,
B	But I must try.
c	Darkness and wind portray
c	Failures of yesterday,
c	Hoping to block my way,
B	But I must try.
d	Steep as the path might be,
d	Please do not hinder me
b	Nor ask me why.
d	I have no surety
B	But I must try.

DIONOL

This form was created by Dion O'Donnell. The rhyme scheme is a–b–c–d–d–c–b–a–b½. The composition is iambic with twelve syllables in each of the first eight lines, and only six in the ninth line. The ninth line repeats the terminal words of the second line. The form is well adapted to dignity, beauty, and art.

*Calkins, *Jean's Journal* (Spring 1969), p. 50.

THE PRICE OF HARVEST

12	a	The harvest cannot come until the fields are plowed,
12	b	The hard crust broken by submission to the steel,
12	c	A bruising and a breaking of the selfish soul
12	d	So that in opened furrows sprouts of love may find
12	d	A soil prepared to nurture growth, enrich the mind.
12	c	The husbandman removes the weeds to bless the whole,
12	b	With soft gentle showers of grace the fissures heal,
12	a	And fruit is the reward, because the heart allowed
6	b½	Submission to the steel.

DIXDEUX (Díx–doó)

As described by Fusco, the Dixdeux, from the French for "ten" and "two," has two unrhymed lines of ten syllables each, followed by a two–syllable line. When used in sequence, the last line often becomes a refrain.* There is no limit on subject matter.

PEACE FOR THE HEART

When the restless heart of man finds content,
we know he has looked beyond himself for
answers.

THE DIXON

This form is named for the poet Richard Watson Dixon (1833–1900), and is taken from his poem "Willow."**It consists of two stanzas of six lines each and a combination of masculine and feminine end words. It is composed in trimeter.

GRAVEYARD OF DREAMS

a	When the heart is crying,
a	And trust is slowly dying,
b	Then do not cling to me.
c	Your promises are worthless,
c	Your anxious jests are mirthless,
b	I canot hear your plea.

---

*Tony Fusco III, "Rediscovering Verse Forms," in Calkins, *Handbook*, p. 25.
**Quiller-Couch, p. 971.

d   The sun is firmly setting,
d   I start a long forgetting
e   To seek a kinder way.
f   Your failures I'll not mention,
f   I'll find my own redemption,
e   My dreams have died today.

DIZAIN

This ten–line form with strict rhyme scheme is a French form.
Untermeyer notes that several were at times brought together as a
kind of Ballade or Chant Royal.* It may be written in tetrameter or
pentameter.**

TO KEEP THE WORLD SANE

a   Say what you will with derision and scorn,
b   Mocking at toilers who follow the plow,
a   Obeying the nudge of the duty-bound morn,
b   Striving as hard as their strength will allow,
b   Earning their bread by the sweat of their brow.
c   Oh, yes, we need dreamers to follow the sun,
c   And singers to sing and jesters to pun,
d   But the practical plodders one must not disdain,
c   For beyond the frivolities, foibles, and fun,
d   They give us the balance to keep this world sane.

THE DOBSON

This form is named for poet Henry Austin Dobson (1840–1924),
and patterned after his poem, "A Garden Song."*** It is composed
of three sets of couplets to a stanza and written in tetrameter.

THE SILENT SPY

a   It is well cats cannot talk;
a   They watch intently as a hawk,
b   Observing with a prowling yen
b   And thoroughness of regimen,
c   For all our private words and sighs
c   Are censored through their queenly eyes.

*Untermeyer, *Pursuit*, p. 191.
**Preminger, p. 197.
***Quiller-Couch, p. 1004.

d	They focus through those amber slits
d	And watch for lapses in our wits.
e	What skeletons, what tales, what pains
e	Are savored in their crafty brains.
f	A lucky thing for us, I vow
f	That all a cat can say is "meow."

DR. STELLA

This eight-line pattern was invented by James R. Gray in honor of Dr. Stella Woodall, who as president of the American Poetry League and editor of the *American Poetry League Magazine* and the *Adventures in Poetry* magazine, is one of our country's greatest contributors to the cause of poetry.

The form is iambic, alternating tetrameter and trimeter. The rhyme scheme is a–b–c–d–a–b–c–d. Lines 2 and 6 have feminine endings.

SEPTEMBER

a	A carousel that gayly spins,
b	Of pinto ponies flying;
c	A dancing bonfire melting frost,
d	And wild geese soaring high;
a	Overflowing granary bins
b	Replace the summer's sighing,
c	An Indian maiden's tresses tossed
d	As fresh winds scurry by.

DODITSU

Fusco describes this Haiku-like Oriental form of nature poetry as possessing an air of conceit in that it was generally used by the upper classes, not gaining in popularity as much as the other Oriental verse forms.* The syllable count of its four lines is 7–7–7–5.

THE CYCLE

Springtime spirit wakes the world,
Summer flexes its muscles,
Autumn gathers its harvest,
Old man winter rests.

*Fusco, in Calkins, *Handbook*, p. 24.

99

THE DONNA

This new form somewhat resembles the Limerick, but the first line of the Donna does not require rhyme. Also unlike the Limerick, the subject matter is of a serious nature. Introduced by Viola Berg, this form features four five–line stanzas. Iambic meter is used. The syllable count and rhyme scheme are noted.

THE LAST RESORT

8	x	When man decides to aid his schemes
6	a	And seeks support from man,
4	b	The help he gets
4	b	Piles up his debts
6	a	And complicates his plan.
8	x	When man in desperation forms
6	c	Committees, trained and skilled,
4	d	Though hope appeals
4	d	The truth reveals
6	c	His goals yet unfulfilled.
8	x	The views of man are limited,
6	e	His strength goes with the years.
4	f	The grandest schemes
4	f	And heroes dreams
6	e	So often end in tears.
8	x	If man at last admits defeat,
6	g	His failures to review,
4	h	And ends his care
4	h	By using prayer,
6	g	He gets what God can do.

THE DONNE

Named for the poet John Donne (1573–1631), this form is taken from his poem "A Hymn to God the Father."* Each stanza contains six lines, the first four of which are written in pentameter, the fifth in tetrameter, and the sixth in dimeter. Rhyming lines alternate, using two rhymes only in the entire poem.

---

*Louis Untermeyer, comp., A Treasury of Great Poems (New York: Simon and Schuster, 1942), pp. 368-69.

WHEREIN IS LOVE?

Wherein is love? May Cupid offer aid?
Can it be fanned from feeble embryo,
Ingredients obtained and craftsmen paid
To add more vital substance to the glow,
And place its fire within a maid?
        Can this be so?

Wherein is love? What color and what shade
Of feeling is emotion, born to grow?
What food, what drink is given to persuade
The power conceived to reach its ultimo,
Assured, emboldened, unafraid
        To overflow.

Wherein is love? Can reason dare invade
The drives and passions pulsing to and fro,
And finally in magnetic escapade,
Exploding in vibrating tremolo.
Will love succumb to barricade?
        I do not know.

DORSIMBRA

This form was designed by three poets from Tennessee — Frieda
*Dor*ris, Robert *Sim*onton, and Eve *Bra*den. The pattern involves
three parts. The first four lines comprise a Shakespearean sonnet
quatrain in iambic pentameter, rhyme scheme a–b–a–b. The second part consists of four lines of free verse. The last four lines are
written in heroic blank verse, the last line repeating the first line.*

THE BURGEONING

From deserts dry and bare my soul must flee
To seek the burgeoning of heart's desire;
To leave the sand, the dry monotony,
And find a way to quench this parching fire,
        Casting off arid chains,
        to search for waiting soil,
        and life-giving water,
        a cleansing, refreshing stream,
A nook where gentle sun will warm and bless
The bursting seed, unshackle it to sprout,
Releasing all my passion and my pain;
From deserts dry and bare my soul must flee.

*The Language Arts Curriculum Guide, Grades 7-12, Memphis City Schools,
Memphis TN, reprinted in *Dorsimbra*, 1976.

DOUBLE BALLADE (See BALLADE.)

DOUBLE CINQUAIN (See CINQUAIN.)

DOUZET

According to Clement Wood, the origin of this recent form is un-known.* It consists of twelve iambic pentameter lines divided into three quatrains, rhymed as noted. As Wood notes, this rhyme scheme is novel in that the concluding quatrain amounts to a summary of the rhyme sounds gone before.

INNER SANCTUM

a   I'm looking for a current linked with mine,
b   And for a knob which I may grasp and turn
b   To pioneer new fields to love and learn,
a   A pastureland of manna, quail, and wine,

c   Where soul can reach to soul in perfect ease,
d   No fences to remove, no waves to part,
d   To find the inner sanctum of the heart,
c   An upward venture, higher goals to seize,

a   To struggle ever onward, to refine
b   The energies, the dross to leave and spurn,
c   For as one reaches for the stars that please,
d   The searching in itself becomes an art.

THE DOWSON

This form is named for Ernest Dowson (1867–1900) and is taken from his poem "They Are Not Long, the Weeping and the Laughter."**Dowson used pentameter in lines 1 and 3 of his two–stanza form, trimeter for the second line, and dimeter for the fourth. Lines 1 and 3 feature feminine endings, and lines 2 and 4 have masculine endings. Rhyming alternates.

*Wood, p. 89.
**Quiller-Couch, p. 1087.

102

WHERE ARE THE JUBILANT?
(A Soldier's Mother Speaks)

Where is the victory amid the crying?
Where is the joy in pain?
Where are the jubilant among the dying?
Where is the gain?

Dearly loved native land, hearts are still yearning,
Deeper than loyalty,
For I am desolate, 'till your returning
My son to me.

DUNI

This form created by Mildred Nye Dewey contains seven lines.
The specific meter and rhyme scheme are given.
Line 1: dactyl, two trochees, iamb
Line 2: three iambs
Line 3: trochee, anapest, two iambs
Line 4: three iambs
Line 5: three iambs
Line 6: four iambs
Line 7: iamb, anapest, iamb
Line 6 introduces a different line of thought which should answer,
complement, or strengthen the message of the first five.

LAND OF THE SUN

a   Warming the prairie, spreading its glow,
b   No shade from burning sun,
c   Reigning in horizon's arc so wide,
a   The lasered sunbeams flow.
c   And melt the countryside ...
b   But I recall when summer's done
a   Its smile on the winter snow.

DUODORA

This form was originated by Dora Tompkins, editor for many years
of the *Nutmegger*, a poetry magazine published in Danbury, Con-
necticut. Her unusual form has two stanzas, the first lines of which
are identical, and the last lines rhyme with each other. The syllable count for each of its seven lines is exact.

IN MY BASKET

A	4	In my basket
x	6	are gathered the items
x	5	I want most to keep,
x	5	the joy of laughter,
x	5	the warmth of a smile,
x	10	the satisfaction of a task well done,
b	10	the sweetness of fellowship I have found.
A	4	In my basket
x	6	is the dew on a rose,
x	5	the wonder of spring,
x	5	the sparkle of snow,
x	5	the magic of love,
x	10	and a sense of humor to ease the load,
b	10	for what I choose, I must carry around.

ELEGY

From the Greek word *elegos,* an elegy is "a lament, a song of mourning, a sorrowful meditation."* Of the many immortal elegies which live in English literature, one of the most notable is Gray's "Elegy Written in a Country Churchyard." Whitman is remembered for his "When Lilacs Last in the Dooryard Bloom'd." This example elegy is a solemn tribute to those who have fought for our country's freedom down through the years.

ELEGY TO THE AMERICAN LEGION

Through the years the legion marches
Led by soldiers in their prime;
Graves cannot contain their spirits,
Halt their feet from keeping time.

Heroes all, our buried brothers,
Parted from their blood and breath,
As the cause for which they battled
Claimed their all, and all was death.

Some came back with scars of combat
Buried deep where none could see,
Finally joining their mute comrades
At the soldiers' reveille.

*Untermeyer, *Pursuit*, p. 193.

Silently across our nation
March their resurrected feet,
Up and down each hill and valley,
Private, sergeant, general, meet.

Fighters to preserve our freedom,
Captains of our triumphs wrought,
All the years our land defending,
All who for our country fought.

What a stalwart, awesome army,
Freed from pain, parading tall,
Issued feet that never tire,
Answering their bugle call.

Those who treasure independence
Owe these men a mighty debt.
Give us ears to hear them marching,
God forbid that we forget.

ENVELOPE STANZA (See QUATRAIN.)

EPIC

Poems of epic quality and stature take time to mature and become
accepted into our literature. No poet can say of himself that he has
written an epic. One definition of an epic is a long narrative poem
elevating a legendary or historical hero by recounting his deeds.
Literature is rich in its vast library of epic poetry, such as Homer's
Odyssey and *Iliad,* Milton's *Paradise Lost,* Dante's *Divine Com-
edy.* The example poem is in honor of the unsung heroines of our
day.* It is written in ballad meter with alternating lines of tetrameter and trimeter.

JOURNEY OF A MOTHER

A new young mother journeyed forth
Upon a summer's day.
"Is the journey long?" she asked her Friend,
And He said she'd find her way
After many a toilsome struggle,
But undaunted and fearlessly
She played with her children all day long,

*Based on an article by Temple Bailey in *Food for Thought,* reprinted in *Streams
in the Desert,* compiled by Mrs. Charles E. Cowman (Grand Rapids: Zondervan
Publishing House, 1966), May 9 entry.

Light-hearted and worry free.
Nothing is better than this, she thought.
Then came the night and the storm,
And the path was dark and the children feared,
But she kept them safe and warm,
And taught them the lesson of holding fast,
And how they could persevere,
Then the mother knew that the night was good,
For she taught them to conquer fear.
The morning came with great steeps ahead,
And they stared at the rocky height.
Then she led the way up each precipice
And showed them the will to fight.
Next clouds of doubt and billows of hate
Bewildered and covered them all,
And the children were hampered by every step,
And were bruised with many a fall.
But with patient wisdom the mother said,
"Lift your eyes from the bitter sod,
And reach for the everlasting light,"
And the mother showed them — God.
The days and the years passed swiftly by
And the journey's end was near,
And the mother grew old and tired and bent,
But the children held her dear.
Her path became a shining road
Which led to a gate flung wide,
And the mother was called to its golden door,
And disappeared inside.
The children watched with faith and love,
With courage and strength of will,
Knowing her spirit would never die,
And her presence was with them still.

EPIGRAM

An epigram is a brief saying which may be merely clever or deeply thought-provoking. The verse form of epigram is usually a couplet, but may be extended into a quatrain.*

*Untermeyer, *Pursuit*, pp. 195-96.

TALE OF A COWARD
(At the Beach)

I stuck in my toes, and backed out again.
The temperature woes sift mice from the men.
I only got wet to my shivering knees,
Retreating to get a nibble of cheese.

EPITAPH

Because an epitaph originally was inscribed on a tombstone, it is brief. At its best, the epitaph is a moving expression of grief. In verse, however, many are light or even cynical.*

Here lies big George
With voice of thunder.
He's finally quiet
Six feet under.

     *   *   *

I toddle now
On heaven's street.
May your pathway
Be as sweet.

ETHEREE

This is a new American unrhymed form originated by Etheree Armstrong. It starts with one syllable in line 1 and increases by one syllable in each line, ending with ten syllables in line 10. The challenge is to have each line end on a strong word, never with a preposition or a conjunction. As editor Calkins points out, the subject matter was originally a phase of immortality, but now includes a variety of topics.**

*Untermeyer, *Pursuit*, p. 197.
**Calkins, *Handbook*, p. 37.

THE GREATEST OF ALL

1 Love
2 cannot
3 die; real love
4 endures all things,
5 forgives and forgets,
6 distributes tenderness,
7 which in turn will never die;
8 bears with all things, hopes for all things,
9 outlives all things, and even outlasts
10 faith and hope. The greatest of all is love.

FIALKA

Fialka is Bohemian for Viola, the form being originated by Viola Gardner.* Non-rhyming, it contains an indeterminate number of lines of nine syllables each. It is composed in amphibrach meter, three feet to the line.

IF . . .

You thrill to the smile of a pansy,
and hear the faint trumpet of lilies,
and understand chatter of sparrows,
and stretch with the corn in its growing,
and cry when the heavens are weeping,
and laugh at the gossip of bluejays,
and hunger with newly-hatched robins,
give heed to the whisper of breezes,
and ache with the dying of roses,
then, you are a lover of nature,
and blessed, richly blessed, in the loving.

THE FLETCHER

Named after John Fletcher (1579–1625), this form is taken from his poem "Away, Delights."**It features a unique combination of long and short lines, the long lines written in pentameter and the short lines in dimeter. The first two long lines in each stanza have feminine endings. The form has two stanzas of eight lines each.

*Calkins, *Handbook*, p. 38.
**Quiller-Couch, pp. 242-43.

108

PILLAR IN THE NORTH
(Inspired by the writings of Jack London)

a The Yukon cold in gray and sunless dawning
b   Tingles the trail.
a The pine and spruce trees, garbed in snowy awning
b   Grown with the gale.
c The subtle gloom surrounding earth and sky
d   With icy breath
c   And muted cry
d Conquers daring travellers with its death.

e Its reign is challenged faintly by a fire,
f   Reviving, warm,
e A stop-gap mercy in a land so dire,
f   Ruled by the storm.
g Who can resist the creeping of its chill?
h   No man can fight
g   Frozen and still,
h A statue in its grip, silent and white.

FOR–GET–ME–NOT

This tiny form, also originated by Viola Gardner, is composed of one couplet, with only four syllables to the line.* Though short, it is titled.

ALWAYS IN FLOWER

Love never wanes
where friendship gains.

FREE VERSE

Free verse has no fixed meter and no rhyme. It is based, rather, on the cadence of natural speech rhythm.** The poetic effect is heightened by imagery and connotative words.

Line length is determined by cadence, the lines ending on a strong word where the voice would ordinarily pause when read aloud with expression.

*Calkins, *Handbook,* p. 39.
**Untermeyer, *Pursuit,* pp. 201-02.

HOLD MY HAND TIGHTLY

Look upon the ocean with me.
Hear the wild waves crashing
upon the rocky shore.
Feel the power of the tide
in its throbbing ebb and flow.
Hold my hand tightly,
for I cannot bear
all this awesome grandeur
by myself.

The breaks between stanzas are determined in the same way as prose paragraphing.

AT EASTER WE REMEMBER ...

How HE changed the whole course
of history,
re-aligned the calendar,
laughed at the horror
of death,
and forever,
and ever,
and ever
wiped away the tears
of despair.

No wonder
we remember,
for when the resurrected Lord
tore the bars away,
we, too,
could hear the glorious notes
of His redeeming triumph
as they echoed all the way
from eternity
to eternity!

FRIEZE

The Frieze, sometimes called the Dicksee, was devised by Olivia Freeman. It contains nine lines structured as given. Composed in iambic trimeter, lines 2, 4, and 8 have an extra syllable because of their rhymed feminine endings.

GOD OF THE SPARROW

6	a	Our Maker lit the sun,
7	b	And tore the void asunder
6	c	By His own willed decree;
7	b	Made wind and rain and thunder,
6	a	Creation had begun;
6	c	From nothing came the sea.
6	a	He's such a mighty One,
7	b	I cannot help but wonder
6	c	How He can notice me.

GARDENIA

Another form attributed to Viola Gardner is the Gardenia, which features ten lines containing two amphibrachs each, with couplet rhyming.

BIRDS OF A FEATHER

A knight and a dragon,
A boy and a wagon,
A girl and a suitor,
A horn and a tooter,
A garden with roses,
And faces with noses,
A sunbeam that dances,
A reindeer that prances;
Like picnics and weather,
These things go together.

THE GILBERT

This form is named after William Schwenk Gilbert (1836–1911), the librettist, so famous for his collaboration on the Gilbert and Sullivan operas, and is patterned after his clever poem "The House of Lords."* Of the seven lines in each stanza, lines 2 and 5 are in trimeter and the remainder are composed in tetrameter. The rhyming scheme is exact.

*Untermeyer, *Treasury*, pp. 956-57.

111

A POEM IS BORN

x   When thinking of what phrase to use,
a   When choosing theme and plot,
b   The agile mind will pioneer
b   And find sweet music for the ear
a   To fill a certain spot,
c   For careful choice and skillful style
c   Will make his effort worth the while.

x   Some words just stumble, some have wings,
d   Some phrases are too slow,
e   And some are frayed from overuse,
e   And some too tight, and some too loose,
d   And some too weak to grow.
f   But with desire to undergird,
f   You'll find your phrase, you'll find your word.

x   So dig for nuggets, poet friend,
g   Sift carefully for gold,
h   Leave stubble, wood, and hay behind
h   And grasp for jewels of the mind,
g   All that your heart can hold.
i   Arrange with grace notes to adorn,
i   And mystically, a poem is born!

HAIKU

The Haiku is a 13th century Japanese form which creates a sharp, simple, rich, concrete image in seventeen syllables. It is described by Harr as an "intuitive response to the Natural world."* It is arranged in three lines of 5–7–5 syllables. Haiku are not titled.

> Orange moon emerges
> over darkening village
> resting on treetops.

Haiku may have fewer syllables.

> Full-blown red rose
> sways in the morning breeze,
> one petal drops.

---

*Lorraine Ellis Harr, ed., *Dragonfly* (July 1976), p. 64. See also Untermeyer, *Pursuit*, p. 205.

TWIN HAIKU

Louise Sipfle put together two Haiku under one title that are in contrast. That contrast should evoke an emotional response in the reader.*

INTERLUDE

During summer rain
frail butterflies find refuge
under rhubarb leaves.

With what delight
anxious wings take flight again
after the shower.

HAIKUETTE

This form is described as the freest, most objective form of poetry in existence. It is composed of three parts, each part a separate entity, yet relative to the whole. There is no syllable count for individual lines, but the total count must not exceed seventeen. The haikuette has no verbs. The poet and the reader must work together in order for the picture and the feeling to be communicated.

INDIAN SUMMER

Clumps of golden asters,
Piles of orphaned leaves,
Bonfire in the dusk.

HAIKU–KU

Having the same structure as the Haiku, its distinct quality is its humor — hence its name. Its brevity lends more to dry humor or light irony. It may be titled. For serious and philosophical treatment of the Haiku form, see Senryu.

TEED OFF

Over the green
into the maddening pond
goes my best shot.

*Calkins, *Handbook*, p. 23.

HAIKU SEQUENCE (Haiku-No-Renga)

A number of related Haiku can be grouped together for combined impact or to cover a sequence. Each Haiku should be able to stand alone.*

A DAY IN A THIMBLE

Yellow canoe
skims silently over
morning ripples.

Dragonflies,
tiny observers,
cruise the water.

Wind blows clouds,
huge ships glide across
distant mountains.

Speedboat churns past
making roller-coaster
for water bugs.

Pine trees
on distant hills
needlepoint the sky.

Birch trees greet wind
waving thousands
of silver banners.

Waning sun ignites
fiery trail across lake,
embers die slowly.

Tiny lighthouse
blinks sleepily
on sand bar.

*Calkins, *Jean's Journal* (August 1974), p. 8.

THE HAUTT

Pronounced "howtt," this form is originated by Viola Berg and is presented in honor of Dr. William D. Hautt, a contemporary Christian educator and administrator of considerable note. This unrhymed form features six lines, has a total syllable count of twenty-two, and has the unusual characteristic of having the syllable count of the first three lines reversed in the second three lines. Each line should end on a strong word. The content should reflect the pursuit of wisdom or the teaching of eternal truth.

IN THE LIGHT OF TRUTH

4	To teach a child
5	to live in the light
2	of truth
2	calls forth
5	joyous hosannas
4	from the angels.

HEROIC COUPLET (See COUPLET.)

THE HERRICK

This form is named after the 17th century poet, Robert Herrick (1591–1674), and patterned after his poem of four stanzas, "To the Virgins, to Make Much of Time."* Although it is not unique with Herrick, he is one of the first to have used it effectively. The use of alternating feminine and masculine end words sets it apart from the usual four–line stanza. Rhyming alternates. Alternate lines are in tetrameter and trimeter respectively.

EVERYWHERE THEY SLEEP
(From the Writings of Philip Freneau)

a	In our fair land where breezes play,
b	Their whispers lullabying,
a	They bless the sod of mound and clay
b	Where Indian chiefs are lying.
c	Beneath the prairie's rolling grass,
d	Where restless wind is sweeping,
c	Tread softly as his grave you pass,
d	For there a brave is sleeping.

*Quiller-Couch, p. 274.

e	Within the forest, lush and green,
f	And on the mountain nesting,
e	Beneath the rock, unknown, unseen,
f	An Indian maid is resting.

g	On hill and valley, ridge and street,
h	Their claim we would not sever,
g	We may be sure beneath our feet
h	Some Indian sleeps forever.

HEXADUAD

This form, devised by Gee Kaye, contains twelve lines, a total of sixty syllables. The syllable count of the last six lines is the reverse of the first six lines. The Hexaduad transposes the first two lines for its last two lines, creating an interesting inversion effect, and bringing the thought of the poem full circle. It is rhymed in couplets.

TO WRITE A BOOK

A	2	To write
A	6	a book is a delight,
b	8	to bless the ones who share the word
b	4	that he has heard,
c	6	the songs he wants to sing,
c	4	that he might bring
d	4	the essence of
d	6	his heart, his soul, his love,
e	4	and make it real
e	8	to those who laugh, and cry, and feel.
A	6	A book is a delight
A	2	to write.

HOURGLASS

Originated by Robert Caldwell, this form is a seven–line poem of free verse containing the syllable line count of 4–3–2–1–2–3–4, which when shaped on the page, resembles an hourglass.*

---

*Calkins, *Handbook*, p. 41. See CONCRETE POETRY.

AGELESS

Faded white hair,
wrinkled brow,
cannot
hide
the smiles
which break through
from her dreaming.

IDENTICAL REFRAIN
(See TERCETS WITH IDENTICAL REFRAIN.)

ITALIAN SONNET (See SONNET, PETRARCHAN.)

JOYBELL

This little form leans toward Concrete Poetry. (See ADDI-TIONAL TOOLS.) Its six lines, with syllable count of 1–2–2–2–4–4, when arranged on the page, resemble the shape of a bell.*

SEA ART

Waves
arrange
pebbles,
driftwood,
and baby crabs
on morning sand.

KALEVADA

The beauty of this form which originated in Finland is in its per-. fect balance. The trochaic tetrameter of the eight unrhymed lines results in feminine word endings.**

CRESCENDO

Time in April merely shuffles,
Days go by with hours dragging.
All the things that seem exciting
Loom ahead with summer promise.
Mystically with passing seasons
Time flows by in faster tempo,
So that in December's waning
Minutes count, each moment precious.

*Calkins, *Jean's Journal* (February–March, 1971), p. 73.
**Calkins, *Handbook*, p. 41.

KERF

The unique arrangement of this form by Marie L. Blanche Adams is in the four groupings of three lines each, with syllable count of 6–7–10, and a strict rhyme pattern.

WITH LOVING FINGERS

a   The master wields his art,
b   Arranging fine stone-chipped bits,
c   Cement and glass, and other worthless things,
a   Each scrap a special part
b   Which with care and skill he fits
c   With loving fingers; and with beauty brings
d   Into burgeoning shape
e   The clear picture in his mind.
c   He sees the symmetry, and genius clings
d   To each feature, each drape,
e   Until the dream he designed
c   Takes life with beating heart and mighty wings.

THE KIPLING

This form is patterned from the first stanza of the poem "L'Envoi" by Rudyard Kipling (1865–1936).* This rhymed form features a combination of anapestic and iambic meter. It also has internal rhyme in the long lines. The effect is very rhythmic.

MY BIT OF SKY

aa   Oh, my inner spirit sings, but alas, I have no wings,
b   And I have no fuel to run.
cc   In some galaxy divine I shall feast on bread and wine
b   For I must reach to the sun.

dd   In my striving I shall find greener pastures for the mind
e   If I waste no time to sigh.
ff   Upward struggle is my right as I champion for light,
e   And to claim my bit of sky.

.

*Quiller-Couch, p. 1071.

KLOANG

The object of this Thailand–originated form is to capture the rhythm of oar strokes. Within each line is a pause (space) between the fifth and sixth syllables. The syllable count in each four–line stanza is 7-7-7-9. In the interweaving rhyme scheme, syllable 5 of line 1 rhymes with the final syllable of line 2 and syllable 5 of line 4. Syllable 5 of lines 2 and 3 rhymes with the last syllable of line 1. The ends of lines 3 and 4 rhyme with each other. Although any subject will do, nature themes are particularly adaptable to this form.

MAN AND A MOUNTAIN

A	B	7	The view is so grand	I stare,
B	A	7	A mountain this fair	is planned,
B	C	7	Extending in air	to be,
A	C	9	The Creator's hand	with awe I see.
D	E	7	I worship and praise	my God,
E	D	7	It's easy to laud	His ways,
E	F	7	His power so broad,	such might,
D	F	9	With homage I gaze	at forest height.
G	H	7	His glory parades	in view;
H	G	7	Majestical clue	persuades.
H	I	7	God's grandeur shines through	His art
G	I	9	And worship invades	my glowing heart.

KYRIELLE

This is an ancient French form made up of quatrains, each stanza ending with a simple refrain. There are eight syllables to the line, the lines rhyming in couplets.*

THE LITTLE COUNTRY THINGS

a	We love the freedom from the crowd,
a	We country folk are strong and proud,
b	We love a telephone that rings,
B	We love the little country things.
c	We love the birds that sing at dawn,
c	The tired rocker on the lawn,
b	The postcard that the mailman brings,
B	We love the little country things.

*Wood, p. 75. See also Calkins, *Handbook*, p. 42.

d   We share a friendly cup of tea,
d   And gather where good friends agree.
b   Our children play with tire swings,
B   We love the little country things.

e   We have our custom and our style,
e   And friends that make life worth the while.
b   Our hearts are free, our spirit sings,
B   We love the little country things.

LADY'S SLIPPER

The interesting feature of this form originated by Viola Gardner is
its use of internal rhyme within each of the three lines. The meter
is iambic trimeter.* The last line should be a springboard for continuing thought, sort of a grace note effect which will leave the
reader in a contemplative mood.

NEVER A SUNSET

Anticipating bliss,
The soul's concluding role,
To fly beyond the sky . . .

*   *   *

WILD OATS OR PUMPKINS

We ought to guard each thought,
We need to plan each deed,
To find the future kind . . .

LAI

Another ancient French form, the Lai is made up of couplets of
five syllables to the line separated by two–syllable lines. Any
number of lines and stanzas may be used.**

*Calkins, *Handbook*, p. 43.
**Wood, p. 88.

BY THE FLICK OF A FINGER

5	a	Seasons bring content
5	a	For their testament
2	b	To man.
5	a	Such magnificent
5	a	Ordered wonderment
2	b	To scan.
5	a	God sends each event
5	a	Since the firmament
2	b	Began.

LANTERNE

Containing half the syllables of a Cinquain, this tiny form was originated by Lloyd Frank Merrell. Basically a nature poem, it is sometimes called a "shaped **whimsey**" because of its whimsical content, and its shape like a Japanese lantern.* No apostrophes are used and each line ends on a strong word. A title is optional.

CAT NAP

1	Warm
2	pussy
3	willows doze
4	in the April
1	sun.

CHAIN LANTERNE

An outgrowth of the Lanterne is the Chain Lanterne introduced by Monica Boyce. The first word of the second Lanterne repeats the last word of the first one, linking them together. The second Lanterne continues and enlarges upon the theme of the first, broadening the idea and lengthening the chain.

*Calkins, *Handbook*, p. 43.

AUTUMN BONFIRES

Through
smoke haze
shines the sun
sinking behind
trees.
Trees
shiver
in the dusk,
their naked arms
bare.

LATIN SONNET (See SONNET, PETRARCHAN.)

LATOVA

Each of the nine lines in this two–stanza form contains seven syllables. It is composed in trochaic tetrameter with one syllable missing in the last foot, making the last foot catalectic. The rhyming is exact.

HYACINTHS

a   Beauty with its vibrant mark
b   Shares its mystery with man,
b   Casts its spell, this artisan,
c   Proving by its every act
c   Nature's marvels are a fact,
c   Apathy cannot distract.
b   Constant in its wondrous span,
a   Throbbing as a dancing spark,
a   Pleasing as a meadowlark.

d   Gardens' rainbow, music's bliss
e   Infiltrate to every part
e   Of the spirit with their art,
f   Bringing loveliness to mind,
f   Harmony to hear, to find,
f   Colors with pure joy designed,
e   Touching wellsprings of the heart.
d   In the soul's analysis
d   Only God could conjure this!

THE LAUREL

Introduced by Viola Berg, the Laurel pairs the stanzas. The first line of stanza 1 rhymes with the first line of stanza 2, the first line of stanza 3 with the first line of stanza 4, etc. Within the stanzas lines 3, 4, and 5 rhyme, as do lines 2 and 6. Lines 2 and 6 are composed in iambic trimeter and are indented. The other four lines are written in iambic tetrameter.

A BRIGHT NEW DAY

a   Ten thousand days have come and gone,
b   With eves and nights among;
c   Each year of days, each passing year
c   Of joys and pain, delight, a tear,
c   Approaches, but to disappear;
b   We are no longer young.

a   But by God's grace from dawn to dawn
d   With patient, loving zeal
e   The Father shapes our busy days,
e   Instructing in His righteous ways,
e   Leading in the paths of praise,
d   His image to reveal.

f   So when the sunset day shall come,
g   The final breath and prayer,
h   From lessons mastered since rebirth,
h   The spirit prospers while on earth,
h   The soul, aware of His great worth,
g   Is more at home Up There.

f   So, roll on, years, though eyes succumb
i   To limitations dim;
j   Departing strength shall not dismay;
j   Praise God, there is a Bright New Day,
j   And He, in love, prepared the way
i   To greater life with Him.

LAVELLE

The Lavelle was originated by Nel Modglin.* This form is composed of couplets and tercets in this order: couplet, three tercets, two couplets. The first and last couplets have the same rhyme.

*Nel Modglin, *The Rhymer and Other Helps for Beginning Poets* (Kanona, NY: J & C Transcripts, 1975), p. 88.

A SONG SO DEEP

How are poems born to men;
Where comes the writing urge, this yen?

A song so deep, a wish, a thought;
Intuitive response, untaught,
A dream awareness which has brought

Such mystic power, it must be heard,
Its spark conspires to undergird
And cries for birth in written word;

For in his lines the poet pours
His soul's beyondness and his lores
That burn into my heart and yours.

His message shaped, he finds release;
With urgings voiced, comes welcome peace.

When inspiration prods again,
Compulsion drives him to his pen.

LIGHT VERSE

Light verse entertains by its light and playful air. Poets of the past have enriched our literary heritage with their witty and scintillating contributions, many times using a mixture of the sly and the solemn, the satirical and even the boisterous, the grave and the gay.* Light verse requires skill and a deft touch. The three examples given show the idiosyncrasies of various situations.

WRITER'S DILEMMA

Seeking for words like a hard driving spy,
Hunting the synonym pages am I,
Ferreting adjectives, sharp-edged and taut,
Digging for adverbs, targeting thought,
Checking the rules of the don'ts and the do's,
Pleading for help from the mythical muse.
While deep in the struggle and heat of the fray,
Fighting for clarity, rhythm, and sway,
I somehow forgot what I started to say!

*Untermeyer, *Pursuit*, pp. 216-17. See also VERS DE SOCIETE.

UNDERSTANDING GAP

One thing youth can't understand
In his to–and–froing,
How his Mom and Dad can be
Delighted with Not Going.

—From *FOR KINDRED HEARTS*

SMALLER THAN A MUSTARD SEED

When to God our prayers aspire,
And He sends our heart's desire,
Our faith was small, we realize,
Because He took us by surprise.

—From *THE HEART OF THINGS*

LIMERICK

One of the prime forms for light verse, the rhythmical Limerick shows off a clever bit of nonsense to beautiful advantage. Its charm comes from "the surprise of the last line, the sudden swoop and unexpected twist of the climax."*

Used by numerous poets, its popularity is based partly on its simplicity. Its five lines are always built on no more than two rhymes (a–a–b–b–a), with the third and fourth lines one foot shorter than the other three.

A nervous young fellow was Willy,
Whose hang-up was really a dilly.
When he got excited
His words came out blighted,
And he ended up thounding tho thilly.

*   *   *   *

A chronic fault-finder was Chedder
Who didn't like bleak winter wedder,
But when the cold waned
He loudly complained
For he didn't like March any bedder.

—From *FOR KINDRED HEARTS*

*Untermeyer, *Pursuit*, pp. 219-22.

CROSS LIMERICK

In this variation created by Ina Mellichamp, lines 1, 2, and 7 have three feet and rhyme with each other. Lines 3, 4, 5, and 6 have two feet and alternating rhyme. The short lines are indented.

PUT

a   A teacher for years was Joe Foot,
a   Who was chided that he'd taken root,
b   But he answered with grace,
c   And with love and good cheer,
b   The classroom's my place,
c   For the Lord wants me here,
a   I have not taken root, I'm just put!

LIMERICK BALLAD

Following the same pattern as the single Limerick, the Limerick Ballad has three stanzas. The first stanza provides the introduction, in the second the action moves along, and the story is concluded in limerick three. A Limerick Ballad contest was sponsored by the Poetry Society of New Hampshire.

THE TALE OF A FROG

There once was a frolicsome frog
Who cavorted about on his log.
    His hobby was eating,
    He always was treating
Himself to the flies in his bog.

To add to the length of this verse,
He decided for better or worse
    To leave his pet bog,
    So he jumped off his log
To hunt for some insects more cherce.

But this venturesome frog from North Skyway
Was hit by a truck on the byway.
    Now his charming wife Joan
    Eats her dinner alone
For his stomach is back on the highway.

LITTLE WILLIE

This distinct little quatrain makes use of a surprise last line with somewhat cruel inflection.* The popularity of this form stems from one of Col. D. Streamer (Harry Graham)'s *Ruthless Rhymes for Heartless Homes.*** This is fun to write, fun to read, and fun for everyone except Little Willie.

> Willie's brother hung him high.
> He dangled there without much hope.
> His mother, hearing Willie cry,
> Yelled "Take good care of Daddy's rope!"

*   *   *

> Willie died. Dad's in a pout,
> Saying things I wouldn't mention.
> Willie he can do without,
> But he wants his tax exemption.

LOGOLILT

This form was originated by Flozari Rockwood,***and features two six–line stanzas composed of lines which depreciate in length. The meter is iambic. The rhyme scheme is given.

"OVER THIRTY" LAMENT

a	8	My mind rejects the latest hit
a	4	If I admit
b	2	I know.
c	8	I meet with patronizing air
c	4	Most everywhere
b	2	I go.
d	8	I am not hep to latest style,
d	4	The youngsters smile,
e	2	But still
f	8	The years will tag them all at last
f	4	And push them past
e	2	The hill.

*Calkins, *Handbook*, p. 44.
**Wood, pp. 92-93.
***Calkins, *Jean's Journal* (Spring 1970), p. 25.

THE LOUISE

This form introduced by Viola Berg may have any number of stanzas. Composed in iambic, the first three lines of each stanza are written in pentameter and the last one in dimeter. Lines 1 and 3 have feminine endings. Lines 2 and 4 rhyme with each other, lines 1 and 3 do not require rhyme.

WHEN I HAVE GONE

x   When I have gone your memory will be counting
a   The little things I did for you although
x   You never seemed to value them as blessings,
a   Some day you'll know.

x   When you must do the things which wait the doing,
b   The undone tasks which haunt each coming dawn,
x   You'll count them then, the many ways I've loved you
b   When I have gone.

LuVAILEAN SONNET (See SONNET.)

LYRA CHORD

This eight–line form was originated by L. Ensley Hutton.* Written in iambic, six lines are in pentameter, and two in dimeter. The "a" lines have internal rhymes, or echoes.

MY COUNTRY, 'TIS OF THEE
(II Chron. 7:14)

a   Oh, Father, lead the way that we might pray,
b   Desert our wicked ways and turn to Thee,
b   To praise Thy name from sea to shining sea.
c   Oh, teach us how
a   To stop our play, in humbleness obey,
c   And do it now,
d   And then, our sorry plight You'll understand
d   Will cleanse our sin and heal our native land.

*Reprinted from *Haiku Highlights* (Sept.–Oct. 1970), pp. 36-37, ed. Jean Calkins, by permission of the publisher of J & C Transcripts. Copyright © 1970. See also *Handbook*, p. 45.

LYRELLE

This form was created by Velta Myrtle Allen Sanford. It may contain two, three, or four stanzas, each written in iambic meter, containing the following structure: line 1, dimeter; line 2, trimeter; line 3, tetrameter; line 4, pentameter. The rhyming alternates. It is adaptable to nature poems and hymns.

MAGIC OF A SUNBEAM

When clouds are near,
And fog has settled down,
What gloom pervades the atmosphere,
And even Mother Nature wears a frown.

What magic lift,
As sunbeams takes the place
Of clouds, a permeating gift,
And all the world then shows a smiling face.

LYRETTE

This free verse form, originated by Dr. Israel Newman, features seven lines, each line ending on a strong word. The syllable count is 2–3–4–5–4–3–2. Balance and beauty are brought forth by the natural cadence of its lines.

END OF A MONARCH

Huge oak,
shocked and torn,
crashed to its knees,
felled by blinding blow
of Jove's lightning,
a giant,
stricken.

LYRIC

A musical, emotional poem with a particularly smooth-flowing, metrical, and rhymed style is considered a lyric. Originally, Untermeyer notes, a lyric was a song sung to a lyre.* Today song writers are known as lyricists.

In this example the rhythmic ballad meter has been used, giving it a sing-song quality.

HOW CAN WE DOUBT

I can trust the God who paints
    The blush upon the flower,
Who makes the diamond dewdrops tremble
    In dawn's magic hour.
I can trust the God who made
    The rippling silver sea.
A God of such magnificence
    Can surely care for me.

I can trust the God who covers
    Valley floors with green,
And tacks his lovely carpet down
    With daisies inbetween,
The God who made the mountains pierce
    The heaven's turquoise skies,
The God who hears the sparrows fall
    Can surely hear my cries.

The God who fuels a million suns
    To light His universe,
And gives the feathered choirs a song
    To joyfully rehearse,
This God whose power goes far beyond
    What mortal eyes can see,
How can I doubt that such a God
    Will take good care of me.

*Untermeyer, *Pursuit*, p. 222.

MADRIGAL

This form, popular in the 14th century in Italy, spread to England in the 16th century. Madrigals were usually set to music and had parts for three or more voices. Thomas Morley popularized this form, and it was again brought into the limelight when Gilbert and Sullivan introduced mock madrigals into their light operas. This rhyming scheme and meter have been copied from a pre-nuptial song in *The Mikado* which begins with the line, "Brightly dawns our wedding day."*

A SLUGGARD AT HEART

a	Promptly, promptly comes the day,
b	Right on time, another dawning.
b	I arise, still sleepy, yawning,
a	Beams of sunlight lead the way.
c	I respond with lukewarm greeting,
c	Not quite ready for this meeting.
d	Where did nighttime hours fly?
d	I stretch and sigh.
e	I would rather snooze instead,
e	Pillow down my drowzy head,
e	Sneak back to my cozy bed,
e	Sneak back to bed.

MANARDINA

This pattern of twelve iambic lines was originated by Nel Modglin.** It combines short lines of four syllables with long lines of eight syllables. Only six of the lines have rhyme.

SECOND THOUGHTS

a	So rash, it seems,
x	Releasing hopes that crowd the heart,
b	To dare to let them fly so free,
b	To think they might come back to me,
x	To bring fulfillment to my soul,
x	That they will last
x	Through winter days;
x	Or will they, dying, withering,
b	Return to mock me hauntingly
b	And laugh; for I, too blind to see
x	Had turned reality away
a	And killed my dreams.

*Untermeyer, *Pursuit*, p. 223.
**Modglin, p. 85.

MARGEDA

This fourteen–line pattern was devised by Edith Thompson, who also designed the Serena. This form is somewhat akin to Robert Cary's Caryotte, but is written in trochaic tetrameter, the last foot catalectic. The lines have both head and tail rhyme in couplets. This form is especially adaptable to the elfin, the grotesque, and the ironic, and to nature poems. This example describes a summer storm.

DRAINING THE CHALICE

High above the cloud banks form,
Sky preparing for a storm;
Dark and heavy is the air,
Mark of lightning's favorite lair;
Waits the earth for needed rain,
Hates its dryness and its pain;
Urges wind to stir and blow
Dirges welcoming the flow.
Clouds build higher, vapors mount,
Shrouds enclose the dripping fount.
Crash! the thunder booms its might!
Slash! the heavens streak with light!
Thor decides to end the dearth—
Torrents drench the waiting earth.

MARIANNE

Another form introduced by Viola Berg is the Marianne which features a unique combination of syllable count and rhyming scheme. Lines 2 and 4 do not require rhyme. The other three lines in each stanza rhyme with each other. The lines are centered on the page.

GUN SHY
(In the Doctor's Waiting Room)

4	a	I am aware
6	x	I am not a bit brave
8	a	And breathe a final frantic prayer
4	x	before I go
2	a	in there.

4	b	I am undone
6	x	And cannot cast away
8	b	the feeling that I want to run.
4	x	I do not think
2	b	this fun.
4	c	I have showered,
6	x	put on my gayest face
8	c	and tranquilizers devoured
4	x	to find I'm a
2	c	coward.
4	d	I guess it's not
6	x	the doctor that I fear,
8	d	but what really bothers a lot
4	x	is the chance of
2	d	a shot.

MEDALLION

This form was originated by Lillian Mathilda Svenson. All lines are trochaic except the last line which is iambic. The form has exact syllable count and rhyming scheme, and is to be shaped on the page.*

WHEN TULIPS BLOOM

x	4	Tulips, blooming,
a	7	nodding, shining heads aglow;
b	8	scarlet, gleaming yellow, swaying
c	7	to a mystic minuet,
c	9	each a captivating bold coquette,
b	10	on my heartstrings delicately playing
a	9	echoed melodies of long ago,
d	7	blessing with a new perfume
d	4	when tulips bloom.

MESSAGE POETRY (See OCCASIONAL POETRY.)

*Calkins, *Jean's Journal* (Oct.–Nov. 1971), p. 19. See CONCRETE POETRY.

METRIC PYRAMID

This form designed by John Milton Smither uses iambic in each
of the meters from monometer to octameter in a–b–b–a–a–b–b–a
rhyme scheme, thus building the pyramid.*

INDEPENDENCE DAY PARADE

2	a	The day
4	b	is clear and bright
6	b	and crowns the thrilling sight
8	a	of marching feet and bands that play.
10	a	The fifes and drums the rhythmic beat obey,
12	b	And decorated floats admiring eyes invite,
14	b	But best of all Old Glory waves in red and blue and white.
16	a	We breathe a little prayer of gratitude, and go our thankful way.

MILTONIC SONNET (See SONNET.)

MINIATURE

This form in trochaic rhythm originated by Margaret Ball Dickson
has become a favorite with many poets. It has an unusual feature
in that the fifth syllable of the first line becomes the first syllable
of the second line. Lines 1, 3, 5, 7, 9, and 10 have seven syllables. Lines 6 and 8 have six syllables and have feminine endings. Lines 2 and 4 have five syllables.** Four of the lines do
not require rhyme.

SYMPATHY BECOMES A CROWN

7	x	Gentleness is born of grief,
5	a	Born of stress and thorn.
7	x	Sympathy becomes a crown
5	a	Only pain has worn.
7	x	Harshness of the inner soul
6	b	Melts with burden bearing.
7	x	Patience earned through struggle's fire
6	b	Molds a love worth sharing.
7	c	Only as we bruise and break
7	c	Can we soothe another's ache.

*Calkins, *Handbook*, p. 45.
**Calkins, *Handbook*, p. 46.

MINUETTE

Introduced by Viola Berg, this form features twelve short lines of four syllables each, divided into two stanzas. Only four of the lines require rhyming. Each line ends on a strong word. Lines 3 and 6 are indented.

IN CLOUD OR CALM

x	There is so much
x	I do not know,
a	I cannot see.
x	But day or night
x	In cloud or calm
a	He watches me.
x	It matters not
x	If storms abound
b	Or if they cease.
x	God knows the way,
x	I'll walk with Him
b	In perfect peace.

NEVILLE

This seven–line poem, originated by James R. Gray in honor of Mrs. Neville Saylor, features a combination of iambic trimeter and tetrameter lines, and has a rhyme scheme of a–b–b–a–c–c–a. Lines 1, 4, and 7 have four feet, and lines 2, 3, 5, and 6 have three feet.

TARGET FOR AN ARROW

You fool nobody with your grin,
Insisting you don't care;
Determined, debonair;
Avoiding friendship's origin.
While ducking Cupid's dart
And covering your heart,
Romance will coyly tiptoe in.

THE NOYES

This form is named for Alfred Noyes (1880–1958), and patterned after his poem "Art"* which features four stanzas of four lines each. Lines 1, 2, and 4 are written in trimeter, and line 3 is in monometer. The rhyme scheme alternates.

DISMISSED!

a	You echo a refrain
b	Of how superb you are.
a	In vain
b	I try to see your star.
c	I'd rather you'd submit
d	Some evidence I know.
c	A bit
d	Of twinkling should show.
e	Why don't you get a yen
f	Ideas to explore,
e	For then
f	You wouldn't be a bore.
g	For hollow words fall flat,
h	A mocking exposé,
g	And that
h	Is all I have to say.

OCCASIONAL POETRY

Occasional poetry is a general term to cover poetic efforts for a specific occasion. Untermeyer observes that traditionally "England's poet laureate is expected to hail the occasion of the queen's birthday with a commemorative poem." In recent years, however, the poet laureate has written public poems on various national occasions.**

Branching out from this idea in a rather broad sense, special occasion poetry can be classified into a number of categories. A brief explanation and an example of several types follow.

*Quiller-Couch, p. 1120.
**Untermeyer, *Pursuit*, pp. 230-31.

CHILDREN'S POETRY

Imaginative writing for children is very rewarding. The subject material and the treatment of the subject are on a child's level. The growing mind is very sensitive to tenderness. Children are not impressed with form, but with rhythm and rhyme and a consistent beat.

GOODNIGHT, WITH LOVE

The little rag doll slept as well as she could
Though her black button eyes wouldn't close,
For her fond little mother had put her to bed,
And lovingly kissed her flat nose.

Then told her a story of fairies that played
On the moonbeams that danced through the trees,
And sang her a song of a crackerjack boat
That sailed on a peppermint breeze.

So the little rag doll slept as well as she could,
But the best she could do was a doze,
For her stuffed little heart pounded loudly with love,
And her black button eyes wouldn't close.

CEASE FIRE

Soldiers are marching all over my bed,
A patrol at the foot and one at the head.
In conflict they think of new tricks to use,
One side will win, and one side will lose.

The pillow's a mountain where they have to go
To check out the valley in the blanket below.
They sneak down the wrinkles, jump over the edge,
Then walk single file on the headboard ledge.

The enemy's trapped, but with courage they fight;
I suddenly feel to take sides isn't right,
So I think that my men fought enough for today,
And with casualties zero, I'll put them away.

COMMEMORATIVE VERSE

Commemorative verse differs from special occasion verse in that an occasion signifies a one-time occurrence, but commemorative verse takes in the scope of historic eras; development, transition, and growth of nations; and particular segments of our national heritage.

TEPEES IN THE TWILIGHT

Tepees in the twilight
Silhouette the sky.
Tethered ponies resting,
Evening breezes sigh.

Toil and battle over
For another day.
Weary braves and warriors
Hang their arms away.

Owls keeping vigil,
Campfires burning low,
Quivered muted arrows
Rest beside the bow.

A mother grieves in silence,
Stifling aching wail.
The son she loved so dearly
Died upon the trail.

Tepees in the twilight
Silhouette the sky.
Warriors dream of glory,
Mothers wonder — why.

MESSAGE POETRY

Sometimes a message in prose will be ignored, but a pointed message expressed dramatically in rhythm and rhyme will accord it a measure of attention, and is as a result both useful and entertaining.

THE PAUSE THAT PAYS

When driving on the highway
In the city or a byway
And the traffic signal turns from green to red,
You'd better stop your jetting
Or morticians will be getting
Another nonconformist who is dead.

With venom you abhore it,
But yet you can't ignore it,
And push your restless foot down to the floor.
You think you might be dashing,
But your future could be crashing.
"Poor Boobie" isn't with us anymore.

There is no way around it,
At least we haven't found it,
So just relax and do not blow your top.
Your brakes are there for using,
And bleeding is confusing,
So when the light turns red, you'd better stop.

SPECIAL OCCASION POETRY

Special occasion poetry is exactly that — a poetic commemoration of an important occasion. It might celebrate a personal event, such as a birthday, or at the other extreme, items of national or international significance.

BOND OF GRIEF
(With reference to
Abraham Lincoln's funeral)

The shrouded horses pulled his bier,
Upon each head a plume,
Their steady hoofbeats joined the dirge
And added to the gloom.

An unbelieving nation mourned,
The bullet's work was done.
It stole their captain's breath away
And pushed him past the sun.

Beneath the sod they laid him down
To start his timeless sleep.
A land still weak from bleeding wounds
Was joined in grief to weep.

SPORTS POETRY

Sports poems must exhibit some aspect of the action, conveyed with enthusiasm, and draw the reader into participation. The first example, using rhythm and rhyme, reflects the excitement of a New Year's Day championship football game, and the second, composed in free verse, brings to life the vivid experience of watching a segment of the Olympics on television.

STAMPEDE OF THE LONG HORNS

What a day, what a thrill, what a game we saw,
Like a thundering herd in a buffalo draw,
The powerful clash when two champions meet,
And the sure advance of the Long Horn feet.

The Texas fans all rejoiced to see
The thorough defeat of Tennessee,
For the best they could do could not compete
With the victory dance of the Long Horn feet.

Excitement ran high through the world of sports,
As voices proclaimed first-hand reports
Of this battling team who could not be beat,
And the touchdown runs of the Long Horn feet.

*   *   *   *

SNOW BIRDS
(At the Olympics)

They burst through the frosty air,
giant stream-lined birds
leaning into the wind.
Their countrymen,
eager-eyed,
watch from the sidelines
and on moving screens back home,
straining every spectator muscle,
nerves tingling in empathy,

holding their icy breath
in an agony of hope,
until the climax
of their skier's graceful flight
brings him suddenly
to earth again,
his gleaming skis
touching the hard reality
of the glassy snow.

Contestant and viewer
breathe again in pained relief
after having been suspended
together
during those
excruciating frozen seconds
of time.

TRIBUTE POETRY

Poetic tributes have been written to honor kings and conquerors, pioneers and adventurers. Poetry lends itself so beautifully to expressions of sentiment, of testimony and admiration.

HE TALKED WITH BIRDS
(A Tribute to Robert Frost)

A man who was acquainted with the night,
Who said that time was neither wrong nor right,
Who went for lonely walks in shining snow,
And knew the hillside when the spring let go,
Who called the sun a wizard, the moon, a witch;
Of nature's secrets was profoundly rich;
A man who stopped to watch the snowflakes fall,
And travelled miles before his twilight call,
Who listened for the thrush's evening cry
And watched for stars to glisten in the sky,
Observed the birches crack their outer sheath,
And wondered at the baby green beneath,
Who talked with bluebird's voice in children's bower,
Conversed with butterflies on tufted flower.
This ageless poet made of life an art
By testing brave ideas in his heart.
The last long leaf has fallen from his tree,
But he revives the spring — in you and me.

OCTAIN

Originated by Lillian Mathilda Svenson, this eight–line pattern has an A–b–c–d–b–c–d–A rhyme scheme and a syllable count of 2–4–6–8–8–6–4–3.* It begins and ends with the same word.

TIME OF FRECKLES

Summer
is a boy thing,
no longer cramped in school,
set free to fish from shady pier,
to climb a tree and pump a swing,
to dive into the pool —
a great career
is summer.

This form is also charming when unrhymed. The syllable count is the same.

TEACH ME TO LOVE

Poet,
teach me to love,
sing tender songs to me.
Lift me above this struggling world,
usher me to clear horizons,
quench the thirst of my heart.
Guide me gently,
dear poet.

OCTAVE

A general definition is simply any eight–line stanza. There is an infinite variety of structures.

One of the most common forms is a pair of quatrains, rhymed a–b–a–b–c–d–c–d.**

*Calkins, *Handbook*, p. 48.
**Untermeyer, *Pursuit*, p. 231.

PRIVATE ANGELUS

a   So gracious is this solitude,
b   As treasured as a long-lost friend,
a   To restless souls, a spirit-food,
b   To hearts, a lovely dividend.
c   No fencing words, congested air,
d   No verbal heights to climb somehow,
c   Just time for loving, time for prayer;
d   A time to be, a time to bow.

An interesting grouping of the octave is two tercets separated by a rhyme pair.*

OUT TO SEA

a   Sea breezes blowing endlessly,
a   The waves in bounding revelry,
a   The tide, in moon-led mastery,
b   Upon the shoreline creeps.
c   Oh, restless sea within my soul,
c   Usurping more and more control,
c   Too soon the ebbing tide will roll
b   And lure me to the deeps.

The poet Swinburne made use of an octave combination in which he mixed feminine and masculine rhymes. He started with a quatrain, added a couplet, and ended with another pair of a–b lines.**

TUMBLEWEEDS

a   So like Mankind, the tumbleweed, surviving
b   But unpredictable, undisciplined,
a   Bereft of roots, and therefore never striving
b   Its wandering, pointless tumbling to rescind.
c   Without a goal or purpose of its own,
c   It flounders on, by gusty breezes blown,
a   Rolling, yes, but never quite arriving,
b   Forever at the mercy of the wind.

*Ibid.
**Ibid., p. 232.

OTTAVA RIMA

This form of the octave was originally used by Boccaccio and other Italian poets. It uses three a–b pairs and ends with a couplet.*

UPON OUR DOORSTEP

a	A new born day is like a fertile field,
b	For we are sowing seeds each hour until
a	The time of golden harvest is revealed.
b	We do not have to look to yonder hill
a	To find an angel's scythe and weigh the yield;
b	The nearest spot might be ours to fulfill.
c	The gleaner in his search for grain to eat
c	Could find life's richest harvest at his feet.

OCTODIL

This is another of the many variations using combinations of the even–syllable lines. The Octodil contains eight unrhymed lines with syllable count of 4–4–6–6–8–8–6–6. Each line ends on a strong word.

A NEW REVEILLE

May our sabers
of troubled today
become plowshares of peace,
digging furrows of love,
resulting in fruit of harvest,
food and drink for a starving world
when the next reveille
bugles, "Brother, awake!"

OCTOSYLLABIC COUPLETS (See COUPLET.)

---

*Untermeyer, *Pursuit*, p. 232.

144

ODE

In Grecian times, Untermeyer reveals, "the ode grew out of a choric song, stately and solemn."* Although there have been various and diverse expressions of the form, poets have preserved the spirit of exaltation, the reaching toward sublimity. The form has ranged from a short two stanzas totaling twelve lines by William Collins in his poem simply titled "Ode," to the lengthy "Ode on a Distant Prospect of Eton College" by Thomas Gray to the ninety-two lines of unrhymed verse with erratic stanza formation used by Alan Tate. What makes an ode an ode, therefore, is not its form but its purpose and the sincerity and intensity of its message.

The example ode has been patterned after Alexander Pope's "Ode on Solitude," using his stanzaic arrangement of three lines of tetrameter followed by a shortened fourth line, and his alternate rhyming pattern.

ODE TO MY CHILDREN

Whatever can I say to you,
My flesh, oh, how can I forget —
You've taught me all your lifetimes through;
    Are teaching yet.

You gave my life its richest days,
With joy I've laughed, with pain I've cried,
And as you've conquered each new phase,
    I've glowed with pride.

When you were little, you were mine,
My privilege to watch you grow,
But when matured, by fate's design
    You had to go.

The world you faced was rough and hard,
Your problem was to find a way.
My spirit bled as you were scarred,
    I could but pray.

I've watched the questing of your souls,
Your struggles in the heat and grime.
I've seen you fall, then grasp your goals,
    And rise, to climb.

You've made my life so full, so deep,
And led me to a long-range view.
I shall not mind as shadows creep;
    I'll live in you.

*Untermeyer, *Pursuit*, p. 233.

OMAR STANZA (See QUATRAIN.)

OPEN COUPLET (See COUPLET.)

ORIGINAL FORM

A category for originality is needed to encourage the reader to experiment with arranging his own thoughts and rhymes as they come naturally. This example is a combination of rhyme and free verse and was not written with any restrictions in mind.

GRANDEUR OF THE SKIES

I saw a ring around the moon.
They say it doesn't mean a thing
except it's going to rain.
Now I disdain
such simple explanations.

How many little stars blew out
their torches in the cosmic night
to form that arc
of purple dark
and make that purple ring?

Whether raindrops fall or not
means nothing to my awe-struck eyes.
I was aware
of God up there,
His grandeur in the skies.

THE O'SHAUGHNESSY

This form is named for Arthur William Edgar O'Shaughnessy (1844–1881), and the pattern is taken from the first stanza of his poem, "Ode."* The four "a" lines have feminine endings and contain three feet. The "b" lines have masculine endings and contain four feet. Only two rhymes are used.

*Quiller-Couch, p. 1008.

MARCHING BAND MYSTIQUE

The band arouses clapping
With its gay, exciting beat,
And many a cane starts tapping,
Martial melodies to greet.
Deft fingers join in snapping
As the crowd enjoys the treat,
And many a foot is tapping
As the drums go down the street.

OTTAVA RIMA (See OCTAVE.)

PALETTE

The name of this form introduced by Viola Berg is indicative of the poem's purpose — to portray a vivid word picture that is painted clearly upon the mind. It should be brief and make use of rhythm and rhyme, but the form itself is not limited in structure. It is the treatment of the content that classifies the poem as a Palette.

BENEDICTION

The winter moon glows mutely down
On all the world below,
Blessing with its friendly light
And beaming on the snow.

PANTOUM

The Pantoum originated in Malaysia to the beat of the tom-tom. It may contain any number of four–line stanzas. The second and fourth lines of each stanza are repeated as the first and third of the following stanza. In the last stanza the second and fourth lines repeat the third and first lines of the first stanza, bringing the theme full circle.*

FOOD FOR THOUGHT

a   I ate so very well tonight.
b   Some little child went starved to bed.
a   I could indulge my appetite,
b   But what of those who have no bread?

*Untermeyer, *Pursuit*, p. 237. See also Calkins, *Handbook*, p. 47.

b	Some little child went starved to bed,
c	While I had more than I could eat,
b	But what of those who have no bread,
c	No shoes to cover little feet?
c	While I had more than I could eat
d	Some orphaned baby cried in vain;
c	No shoes to cover little feet,
d	No sustenance for hunger pain.
d	Some orphaned baby cried in vain,
e	Stark hunger in his eyes was traced,
d	No sustenance for hunger pain,
e	He could have lived on food I waste.
e	Stark hunger in his eyes was traced.
a	I could indulge my appetite.
e	He could have lived on food I waste,
a	I ate so very well tonight.

PARODY

Parody, the imitating or mimicking of the work of another, is as old as poetry itself. Generally, it can be of two types — comic parody, which is close to burlesque, and literary or critical parody, which imitates more closely the parodied author's style.

Parody, while it can be ironic, sarcastic, or even sometimes malicious, provides, nevertheless, a healthy relief from pompousness, solemnity, self-importance, or even pronounced stylism. It is probable that it originated as an emotional relief to tragic themes in classical drama.*

NEVERMORE

I've been Edgar Allan Poe–ing, till my mind is slowly
going
As I've meditated ruefully upon this tearful lore.
I have put up with his rappings and his ghostly
knuckle tappings,
The intruding of his wailings as they filter through
my door
And his weird and slinking shadows playing strangely
on my floor,
None of which I'd known before.

*Preminger, p. 600.

As his spell on me was growing, I could hear his
    raven crowing,
And I must admit I'd never heard a raven's voice
    before,
So I sat there, breath abated, and in expectation
    waited,
But his words were disappointing — all he said was
    "Nevermore,"
While poor Edgar longed for greetings from his
    wandering lost Lenore.
Could he not have chortled more?
After dire mood abetting in this strange fantastic
    setting,
Why pick a tongue-tied raven to perform this vital
    chore?
Yet the ancient bird he's using croaks a word just
    plain confusing.
I'm through with ghosts, and dreams, and spells, and
    shadows on my floor —
He'd better find a better way to find his lost Lenore —
I've had it — Nevermore!

Parody may ape reasoning and mood rather than style. This next example quotes famous couplets of the witty and prolific Richard Armour, one of the most successful contemporary light verse writers.

A FOUL SITUATION

Richard, Richard, do you hear,
Though your quip we hold quite dear:

"When eggs are eighty cents a dozen
It pays to have a country cousin."*

All we can do now is holler
For the price is past a dollar.
Generous, cousins just can't be
With hungry cityfolk like me.
Though their giving's quite extensive,
Eggs are just too plain expensive.
Save my paycheck, borrow, beg,
I just can't conjure up an egg.
Since these prices make me sicken,
Guess I'll make friends with a chicken.

*By permission of Richard Armour.

PETRARCHAN SONNET (See SONNET.)

PENDULUM

This eight–line poem was created by Etta J. Murphy, featuring graduated line lengths of 8–6–4–2–2–4–6–8 syllables, with rhyming couplet.*

FLASH OF A JEWEL

Each day, another front row glance,
another shining chance;
the minutes glow
and flow
so fast,
I am aghast;
their gleams I cannot hold,
each gem is gone, too soon, too old.

PENSEE

This pattern originated by Alice Maud Spokes has no rhyme, but has exact syllable count for its five lines, each of which ends on a strong word.**

SKY BALLET

2	Winging
4	over green mist,
7	lapping waves and tide-washed sand,
8	the graceful seagull dips and soars,
8	a vision in pearl gray feathers.

THE PHILLIMORE

This form is named for poet John Swinnerton Phillimore (1873–1926), and is patterned after his poem "In a Meadow." *** It combines pentameter and dimeter lines in an eight–line stanza, and is rhymed in couplets.

*Calkins, *Haiku Highlights* (July–August, 1970), p. 55.
**Calkins, *Handbook*, p. 48.
***Quiller-Couch, p. 1102.

GRIST FOR THE WASTEBASKET

a   Maybe today
a   A long awaited check will come my way.
b   Anticipation is so very sweet,
b   And I repeat
c   Some editor will send some word, I know,
c   And then — the blow.
d   Signs of disappointment are detected —
d   I'm rejected!

POULTER'S MEASURE (See QUATRAIN.)

QUATERN

This ancient French form features four stanzas composed in iambic tetrameter, using only two rhymes. The first line of stanza 1 is used as a refrain line, occurring as the second line of stanza 2, the third line of stanza 3, and the last line of stanza 4. The rhyme alternates to accommodate the refrain. The theme line fits smoothly into the message.

GIVE ME ANOTHER DAY

A   Please, Time, give me another day,
b   Adjust your onward force to "slow"
a   For I must find a chance, a way
b   To right some wrongs of long ago.

b   So many kindnesses I owe;
A   Please, Time, give me another day,
b   For I have seeds of love to sow
a   And many words of love to say.

a   I want to learn to trust, to pray,
b   To see my seedlings sprout and grow;
A   Please, Time, give me another day
b   For fruits of righteousness to show.

b   It's taken years for me to know
a   The transient value of this clay;
b   I understand it now, and so —
A   Please, Time, give me another day.

QUATRAIN

Untermeyer observes that "the quatrain is the most prevalent unit of English verse."* Basically it is a four–line unit, arranged in any scheme.

BALLAD STANZA

Originally the quatrain evolved from the seven–foot iambic lines of ballad meter. Thus the x–a–x–a rhyme scheme and 4–3–4–3 syllable count.

FROM YESTERDAY'S CORNERS

x   My dreams are never predesigned,
a   Nor logic do they borrow,
x   But in some mystic silent way
a   They border on tomorrow.

ENVELOPE STANZA

Other rhyme schemes include the a–b–a–b pattern, the less familiar a–b–b–a called the Envelope Stanza, the single rhyme a–a–a–a, and the couplet pattern, a–a–b–b. The example poem illustrates all four varieties.**

SUN, MOON, AND STARS

a   When the morning sun awakes
b   And spreads its cheer through waiting hours,
a   What a change the sunshine makes
b   As bashful buds turn into flowers.

a   Higher, higher, goes the sphere
b   And quickened is the pilgrim's pace.
b   The sun beams everywhere to grace
a   The deepest vale with noontime cheer.

a   Through the waning hours of day
a   Our sun slips gradually away,
a   And leaves in glorious array
a   To gladden hearts while yet it may.

a   The twilight settles over all
a   Before the nighttime shadows fall.
b   While stars and moon their vigil keep,
b   A tired world drops off to sleep.

*Untermeyer, *Pursuit*, p. 255.
**Untermeyer, *Pursuit*, pp. 255-57.

OMAR STANZA

An iambic pentameter pattern rhymed a–a–x–a was popularized by Fitzgerald in the *Rubaiyat of Omar Khayyam.**

AT THE RAINBOW'S END

a   Oh, come with me beyond the clouded sky,
a   A place untouched by human greed or sigh,
x   And know the promise at the rainbow's end,
a   Where friend meets friend and never says goodbye.

POULTER'S MEASURE

A form of the quatrain used extensively in hymns features shorter line lengths of 3, 3, 4, 3 iambic feet, identified as SHORT METER. In the 16th century this was known as Poulter's Measure.** Any rhyme scheme may be used. This example uses the ballad stanza form.

ONE OF HIS TRINKETS

I raise my awe-struck eyes
To view a redwood tree.
Such overwhelming magnitude
Reveals my God to me.

COMPLETE QUATRAIN

A complete quatrain expresses a complete thought in its four lines, and is not part of a longer poem. See the four single examples given above. A number of other examples are elsewhere in this book.

QUINNETTE

Originated by Ethelyn Miller Hartwich, the Quinnette contains two five–line stanzas, rhymed a–a–b–a–a and c–c–b–c–c. Lines 1, 2, 4, 5, are written in trochaic tetrameter, line 3 is in trochaic trimeter. This form is designed for the elfin or humorous or for nature themes.

*Untermeyer, *Pursuit*, p. 257.
**Wood, p. 43.

HER NAME IS EVE
(Temptation)

Played with sometimes, yet unbid,
Always lurking near, and mid
    Off-guard hours she calls,
Teasing, laughing, partly hid;
Tripping me into a skid.

Trapped again! Lured by her spell,
Sugar-coated bit of hell;
    Caged within her walls,
Sternly to myself I tell —
Next time, wear your armor well!

QUINTANELLE

Originated by Lyra LuVaile, another five–line form uses the combination of a couplet followed by a tercet. The syllable count is 10–10–4–6–10, making lines 1, 2, 5 pentameter, line 3 dimeter, and line 4 trimeter. Each stanza is composed of one iambic sentence.

VAGABOND SKY

The wind is luring toward adventure road
Which beckons me and dares me to unload
    My careful plans
    And my allotted spans
To find excitement in some far off lands.

I hear the whisper; wondering, I wait
To think it over, ponder, hesitate —
    My cozy chair
    I try to gauge, compare
My life at home with what is offered there.

I wonder if the wind would show the way
Where love would greet me at the close of day,
    Or is the breeze
    A tantalizing tease
Which tries to route me from my life of ease?

Oh, gypsy winds that tempt and tease and lure,
I'd rather stay where love and peace are sure,
For now I find
That I am disinclined,
But try again, for I could change my mind.

QUINTET

Written in a variety of rhyme schemes, metric structures, and line lengths, the quintet is, simply, a five–line stanza. See the following forms for examples using five–line stanzas: Quinnette, Quintanelle, and Quintette.

Although many of the quintet forms are unlisted in many textbooks, they have been used by such poets as Donne, Shelley, and Sir Thomas Wyatt. The quintet with unrhymed last line, illustrated below, was used by a number of poets, including George Herbert.*

TO LOVE AND TO KEEP

America, the land the pilgrims sought
That conscience might be free,
At price of hardship with their life-blood bought,
A heritage for you and me
To cherish.

Robert Browning favored the a–b–a–b–a rhyme arrangement in his poem "The Patriot."**

HELICOPTER WINGS

The perfume which the purple lilac brings,
The magic captured in the prismed dew,
A hummingbird with helicopter wings,
How thrilling is an hour spent with you.
What blessings come from joy in little things.

*Untermeyer, *Pursuit*, p. 258.
***Ibid.*

QUINTETTE

This five–line form of three stanzas, created by Fay Lewis Noble, has the interesting feature of using the first line of stanza 1 as a key line, which is repeated as line 3 in stanza 2, and concludes the poem in line 5 of stanza 3. Stanzas 1 and 3 are composed in iambic pentameter, but in stanza 2 only the middle line is pentameter. Lines 1 and 5 are composed in iambic dimeter, and lines 2 and 4 in iambic tetrameter. Because of the refrain in the center of stanza 2, the rhyming scheme deviates to go around it.

SHUT OUT THE MOONLIGHT

A	Shut out the moonlight from my memory.
b	The years have only added to the gleam
a	Of Luna's power, as it endlessly
b	Entices from the past each buried dream,
b	And ghosts them past the dry bed of my stream.
a	It mocks at me,
c	And boldly dances through the trees.
A	Shut out the moonlight from my memory,
c	And close the folding shutters, please.
a	It shall not see
d	The tears that fight their way unbid to fall
a	Cascading in nostalgic reverie.
d	I only ache when I relive it all.
a	Just let me drink my lonely cup of tea.
A	Shut out the moonlight from my memory.

RENGO (See TANKA.)

REPETE

This form is similar to the French Rondel in that lines 1 and 2 are repeated as lines 7 and 8 and lines 13 and 14. In this form, however, the wording in the refrain need not be identical. The first stanza has eight lines, the second, six. Only two rhymes are used.* The example is written in iambic tetrameter.

*Calkins, *Handbook*, p. 26.

A WISHING STAR

A	I saw a star fall from the sky
B	And streak across the purple night.
a	In transfixed wonderment stood I,
b	Agape at such an awesome sight.
a	A chance to wish was blazing by,
b	And I was stunned in pure delight
A	To see a star fall from the sky
B	And streak across the purple night.
a	What made it burn? What made it fly?
b	What mystifying heavenly rite
a	Declared that it should burn and die
b	In bursting torch of amber-white?
A	I saw a star fall from the sky
B	And vanish in the purple night.

RETOURNELLO

Composed of two or more stanzas, this form was originated by Flozari Rockwood. Lines 1 and 4 of each stanza repeat, but may be slightly different to emphasize the thought. The rhyme pattern and syllabication are noted.

I WOULD NOT BE A WEED

4	a	I would not be
6	b	a weed when threshing's done,
8	b	so that of fruit I would have none,
4	a	but I would be
4	c	a full ripe ear
6	d	of tasseled corn instead,
8	d	for there are hungry to be fed,
4	c	a seedcorn ear.

RHYME ROYAL (See SEPTET.)

RHYMED CINQUAIN (See CINQUAIN.)

157

RIPPLE ECHO

This unusual form, originated by L. Ensley Hutton, begins and ends its stanzas with rhyming ripple and echo couplets which must be aligned on the page. The form is composed in trochaic tetrameter, catalectic; the longer lines contain seven syllables, the echoes three. The four intermediate lines also have couplet rhyming. No punctuation is used other than an exclamation point at the end of the echo lines.

MAN IS JUST A DOT

Teach us, Lord, how small we are
                        from a star!
Whirling round the atmosphere
Earth a constant circuiteer
Bound by laws so forceful, strong
Keeping us where we belong
Just one planet out in space
                        by Thy grace!

Science pioneers a trail
            heights to scale!
We are awed by magnitude
And in fairness must conclude
God is great, and we are not
Little man is just a dot
Worship then becomes an art
                        from the heart!

RISPETTO

The Rispetto is an Italian form which consists of two or more stanzas with different rhyme schemes. Its length is almost always eight lines, divided into two quatrains, rhymed a–b–a–b; c–c–d–d.*

THE CHANCE TO ERR

Our youth seem doomed to join in common fate,
To doubt the lasting worth of parents' ways,
Their standards and their goals to tolerate,
Their attitudes consigned to "olden days."

Advice well-meant from kindly wiser tongue
Seems lost upon the sprouting greening young.
Sometimes they badly need the chance to err
To see how very right their parents were.

*Wood, p. 89. See also Calkins, *Handbook*, p. 52.

RONDEAU

The Rondeau, another popular French form, is made up of thirteen lines plus a refrain, and is divided into three stanzas. The refrain appears at the beginning of line 1 of stanza 1 as well as the concluding line of stanzas 2 and 3. Only two rhymes are used.* Poets have composed Rondeaus in tetrameter and pentameter. This example is written in pentameter.

OH, CHRISTIAN, SING!

Ra	Oh, Christian, sing, and heav'nward praises fling
a	With joy to make the courts of heaven ring.
b	Lift up your voice that all mankind might see
b	The greatness of His sovereign majesty,
a	And worship Him, our Prophet, Priest, and King.
a	Arouse the sleeping world to wakening,
a	To see God's ways, His purpose fathoming,
b	Before His throne to bend on humble knee.
R	Oh, Christian, sing!
a	All kindreds and all tribes of earth shall bring
a	Hosannas and their homage, publishing
b	His magnitude, supreme epitome,
b	His greatest crowning triumphs yet to be,
a	The final glorious time of harvesting.
R	Oh, Christian, sing!

RONDEAU REDOUBLE

The Rondeau Redouble has a set pattern of its own and is not merely a Double Rondeau. The six stanzas of quatrains and final half-line refrain are all based on two rhymes. The opening quatrain establishes the pattern and thought. Each of its four lines is repeated as the final line of the next four stanzas. The last line of the sixth quatrain is new, but it is followed by a repeat of the first half of line 1 of the poem.**

*Untermeyer, *Pursuit*, p. 268.
**Untermeyer, *Pursuit*, pp. 271-72.

A ROBIN'S SONG

A   A robin's song has wafted through to me,
B   My heart is blessed with chorus of content.
a-1 No gloom can long withstand such jubilee,
b-1 New hope awakes with touch of wonderment.

b   Such joyous notes are far more eloquent
a   Than man can make with all his mastery.
b   My cares are gone, and every vague lament,
A   A robin's song has wafted through to me.

a   If feathered creatures weave such symphony,
b   How can this mortal be indifferent.
a   They sing their own enchanted melody,
B   My heart is blessed with chorus of content.

b   A robin's trill is so magnificent,
a   It far surpasses in its purity
b   The harmonies which able men have blent,
a-1 No gloom can long withstand such jubilee.

a   So sing, oh, robin, in your cherry tree
b   To this most grateful awed recipient.
a   Thrill me with your throated majesty,
b-1 New hope awakes with touch of wonderment.

b   My soul is fed and spirit smiles consent,
a   Treasured is your brand of psalmody.
b   Your therapeutic lift is excellent,
a   And I will always hear in memory
A½   A robin's song.

RONDEL

A 14th century French form, the Rondel was given its present form of fourteen lines on two rhymes by Charles d'Orleans. The first two lines are repeated in the seventh and eighth, and again in the final couplet.*

*Wood, p. 78. See also Calkins, *Handbook*, p. 53.

A POET SINGS OF LITTLE THINGS

A   A poet sings of little things
B   And makes them beautiful for me,
b   Of spring's first breeze and April's glee,
a   A cricket on the hearth that sings,
a   Of eagle fledglings trying wings,
b   And stars that twinkle joyously.
A   A poet sings of little things
B   And makes them beautiful for me.

a   The thrill that Christmas morning brings,
b   Of hearts that love so tenderly,
b   The angel's song of ecstasy,
a   Nostalgic bells that memory rings.
A   A poet sings of little things
B   And makes them beautiful for me.

RONDELAY

This seven-line form has the same rhyme scheme as the Rondelet. Its syllable count is 4–4–4–4–8–8–4, and it is rhymed A–b–A–a–b–b–A.* Lines 1, 3, and 7 are the same.

TO GOD BE THE GLORY

God shall have praise,
  Resoundingly
God shall have praise,
  His name to raise.
His ransomed join the jubilee
And even rocks and stones agree
God shall have praise.

RONDELET

The Rondelet contains seven lines in each stanza. The rhyme scheme is the same as the Rondelay: A–b–A–a–b–b–A. The difference is in the line syllable count, which is 4–8–4–8–8–8–4. The refrain lines, 1, 3, and 7, are in dimeter. The other lines are composed in tetrameter.**

*Calkins, *Handbook*, p. 54.
**Wood, p. 81. See also Calkins, *Handbook*, p. 54.

I MUST HAVE GOD

I must have God
To be my joy from day to day.
I must have God
To lift me from the earth and sod,
For me to love, to whom I pray.
For me, there is no other way,
I must have God.

ROSEMARY

This twelve–line poem is composed in pentameter, opening and closing with a couplet, with two envelope quatrains in between. The "c" and "e" lines are indented.

BEAUTY IS

a   That which gives the doubter a reprieve
a   And gentles understanding to believe,
b   An essence promptly claimed, yet unpossessed,
c   A force which needs no fist, no mighty arm,
c   Which melts the opposition with its charm;
b   Just being, it is stronger than the rest.
d   A pulsing inner harmony to feel,
e   Its influence a blessing and an art,
e   Which links the joys and teardrops of the heart,
d   So tender is the touch of its appeal,
f   A magic spell which woos with pure delight,
f   Which starts with longing, ending out of sight.

ROUNDEL

This form was adapted from the Rondeau by the English poet Swinburne. The refrain in lines 4 and 11 is repeated from the opening words of line 1. The refrain is a "b" rhyme; only two rhymes are used.*

*Untermeyer, *Pursuit*, p. 274.

COME, FLY WITH ME

A	Come, fly with me to fairyland
b	Where genies wait impatiently
a	To guide your unbelieving hand.
A½	Come, fly with me.
b	Wishes bloom there on a tree,
a	And dreams come true upon demand,
b	Where nectar flows unendingly
a	From moonbeams tied to silver strand.
b	Mermaids waltz in sequinned sea,
a	And pixies dance on magic sand.
A½	Come, fly with me.

THE RUSSELL

This form is patterned after George William Russell's (1867–1935) poem "The Great Breath."* It features three stanzas, using a combination of pentameter and trimeter. Alternate lines rhyme. The short lines are usually indented.

THE FINAL BEACON

a	There is a narrow road for all to find;
b	Travelers long to leave the thorn and briar,
a	A shadowed path, its winding course designed
b	To lead the spirit higher.
c	There is an inner voice which all may hear,
d	Whose influence of comfort shall not cease,
c	For loving words of healing cast out fear,
d	And bring the weary peace.
e	There is a light when fueled by a prayer,
f	A beacon for the tired souls that roam,
e	When joined with faith, its glow becomes a flare
f	And guides the pilgrim home.

*Quiller-Couch, p. 1084.

SACRED SIGNIA

This ten–line pattern utilizes pentameter and dimeter line lengths and an ending couplet. Only three rhymes should be used.

FOR ALL YOU ARE

a	What do I have that I might offer you
b	For all you are?
a	You walk with me and see my troubles through
b	And guide me far,
c	Much farther than I'd dare to go alone,
b	To find a star,
c	And even grasp some moonbeams for my own;
c	You are my strength, my faithful cornerstone.
a	I haven't much, my heart, of course, you knew,
a	And all my love, and, yes, a rhyme or two.

SAGA

The saga comes from 12th and 13th century Norway and Iceland. The tales of adventure, historic or legendary, were transmitted orally for centuries until finally recorded by scribes.* It has come to mean a long narrative poem.

This example evolved from the parable of the canyon by Ralph Connor.** It is a saga of how the canyons came to be and of the delicate flowers which grace their deeps.

SAGA OF THE FLOWERS

A minstrel sang to the passersby
Of a time when the prairie was king,
And the earth was like a great broad plain
And the meadowlarks would sing.

One day the Lord of the Prairie appeared
And could find no flowers at all.
And the plain regretted she had no blooms;
On the birds did the Master call.
He asked them to carry the life-filled seeds
And to fling their stamen wide.
The lilies and crowfoot and sunflowers grew
And became the prairie's pride.

*Untermeyer, *Pursuit,* p. 276.
**In "Mountain Trailways," reprinted in Cowman, May 25 entry.

The Master came and was pleased with the bloom,
But some of His favorites He missed,
The columbine and the violets and ferns,
And clematis the dew had kissed.
With sorrow the prairie told her tale,
How the winds blew the seeds away,
And how some of the flowers could not live
In the heat of the shadeless day.

The Master commanded the lightning flash
And the elements parted and swooned.
The prairie rocked and groaned in pain
From the new-felled gaping wound.
The rivers poured waters into the deeps,
Depositing fertile mold.
Again the birds scattered precious seed,
All each chasm and furrow could hold.

After a time the rocks were decked
With mosses and trailing vine.
The violets and maidenhair grew in the clefts,
And blossomed with columbine.
It became the Master's favorite haunt,
He loved these flowers so,
But they needed a crevice rough and deep
Before their seed could grow.

So traveller, when your canyon comes,
Don't fear the shade and the fall.
You'll find it has fragrance the prairie lacks
And the sweetest flowers of all.

SAN HSIEN (three strings)

This little form, originated by Jessamine Fishback, contains ten lines written in iambic dimeter. The first line begins with a rest, as in music. The rhyme scheme is A–B–b–a–c–c–a–b–B–A. The first two lines are repeated in reverse order at the end of the poem.

LOVE IS BORN

A	.... Love is born,
B	so pure, so new,
b	and bashful, too,
a	so fresh, unworn,
c	to grow, to swell,
c	to weave its spell
a	afresh each morn,
b	to rendezvous;
B	so pure, so new,
A	our love is born.

SAPPHICS

This unrhymed ancient stanzaic form was derived from the works of Sappho, the poet of Lesbos.* The type of metrical pattern which bears her name consists of four–line stanzas of somewhat erratic meter; the first three lines are long, the final line is short. Edgar Pangborn, in "Sapphics for Icarus," used feminine endings for the long lines followed by a masculine ending. The example follows his form.

THE ETERNAL BEAT

Each newborn mortal unknowingly mounts the treadmill
Starting with instinctive infant breathing.
A force much deeper than his conscious being
    marches him on.

The turbine never stops and never tires;
The belt propelled in silent steady cadence
Leads inevitably to the far side of the valley
    and a new drum.

SATIRE

Satire is defined by Webster as "a literary work holding up human vices and follies to ridicule or scorn."**Its tone changes from poet to poet. "Horace's satires are gentle, Juvenal's are scarifying, Dryden's are solemn, Pope's are biting, Byron's are almost blithe."***

This example of light satire reveals the weakness of human nature in our susceptibility to deceit.

*Untermeyer, *Pursuit*, p. 276.
***Webster's New Collegiate*, 7th ed., s.v. "satire."
***Untermeyer, *Pursuit*, p. 277.

A FINE KETTLE OF FISH

In these days of confusion and guessing
When truth is a hard–to–find blessing
By hit and by miss
We've now come to this
The yes–men aren't sure what they're yessing.

SCALLOP

Marie L. Blanche Adams' form is composed of three related six–line stanzas written in iambic. The lengthening and shortening of the lines gives an ebb and flow effect. The stanzas may be separated if the thought is complete in itself. In this example the idea flows directly from one stanza into the other. Each new grouping of six lines has a new rhyme scheme.

MIRACLE OF THE RAIN

2	a	The rain
4	b	carressed the earth
6	c	with loving prismed tear,
6	c	glistening pure and clear
4	b	beyond all worth.
2	a	The lane
2	d	washed new,
4	e	with freshness dripped,
6	f	and eager blossoms showed,
6	f	their eager faces glowed
4	e	and gently sipped
2	d	the dew,
2	g	while I
4	h	reached down to stare
6	i	at beauty so intense,
6	i	at such magnificence,
4	h	how could I dare
2	g	pass by?

SEAFONN

Originated by Elizabeth Maxwell Phelps, the name Seafonn comes from the Anglo-Saxon for seven. Its seven lines are rhymed a–b–c–c–b–a–a. It is written in iambic tetrameter but lines 2 and 5 are catalectic.* The thought pattern presents an argument or a state of affairs in the first five lines, which is answered or counter-balanced in the final couplet.

*Calkins, Handbook, p. 55.

TO A TEDDY BEAR

a   I'm left alone, and I am blue,
b   Without my playmate buddy.
c   Now he is four, he knows the rule;
c   And he has left for nursery school
b   To play, and learn, and study.

a   So bide your time the hours through,
a   For he'll be back at half past two.

SEDOKA

This Oriental verse form consists of six lines having syllable counts of 5–7–7–5–7–7. The poem is usually broken into two stanzas, but may be run together. The content of the first three lines is similar to the Haiku, dealing with some observation of nature. The last three lines provide an interpretation.*

THE WINGED ONES

Once more the wild geese
heed that call to southward flight,
heading across unmapped miles.

Beyond reasoning,
man, too, hears a strange command
to go to a far country.

SEDOKA-HOKKU

This is a series of related Sedoka.**This example is in the nature of a double Sedoka in which the observation is followed by an analogy.

TIME OF SHEAVES

Tingle in the air,
the last apple stored away,
ripe, rich tint in the cornfields;
sharp October sun
watches over the harvest;
one by one, the fields rest.

*Fusco, in Calkins, *Handbook*, p. 24.
***Ibid.*

Man contemplates his
labors of a long summer,
hoping for autumn plenty.
Each man, a farmer,
gathers his weeds with his crops,
and finds mice in the seedcorn.

SENRYU

A Senryu has the same unrhymed form and syllable count as the Haiku (5–7–5, or less), but in content it relates to people, to our human-ness in nature, to our relationships with each other, our foibles, weaknesses, and idiosyncrasies. Senryu involve human reactions and responses, relating man as he is.*

This brief form can contain only the essence of a truth as the poet sees it or as he ties a truth and an experience together. Philosophy, emotion, beauty, and impact must all be unified in some measure so that the combination offered is thought-provoking, a mirror by which man can in some way see himself.

Hearts that are brittle
resist tenderness and love
fearing they will break.

SEOX

Seox is Anglo-Saxon for six. Sometimes spelled "siex," the form was fashioned by Ann Byrnes Smith. This little free verse pattern has a total of twenty-eight syllables, with the following syllable count in its six lines: 3, 7, 6, 5, 4, 3.**

LITTLE BOY LOST

Toy soldier
waits in the quiet attic
for the remembered touch
of little fingers
to resurrect
life again.

*Harr, p. 65.
**Calkins, Handbook, p. 56.

169

SEPTANELLE, SEPTET

SEPTANELLE

This seven–line poem created by Lyra LuVaile combines various line lengths, has its own rhyme scheme, and is centered on the page.

TO SING ANOTHER DAY

4	a	Man looks away
6	b	from self and garb of brown
10	a	up to the throne of grace, and there to lay
4	b	his burden down,
6	c	for in the upward swing
10	c	he gains momentum and the hope to sing
4	a	another day.

SEPTET

Although the seven–line stanza is rather uncommon, "it has been employed with subtle variations by a number of poets." The possible rhyming combinations involving seven lines are many. This first example follows the rhyme pattern and line length used in Thomas Traherne's "Eden."*

THE TEARS ARE SINGING

a The chorus chimes, sound barriers to part;
b It is not news
b That raucous chords will bruise
a The finely tuned and music loving heart.
b Some notes the spirit cannot use.
c The purest songs induce the soul to weep;
c The theme is mute — its crying is too deep.

An entirely different rhyme arrangement was used by Robert Browning in the first stanza of "Misconceptions."

TWO MASTERS

a A battle raged within today,
b For ego-Self was paining,
a As Soul was losing in the fray
b And selfish Will was reigning.
b I halted then, disdaining
a My dual nature to survey.
a My Id said, "fool"; my Soul said "pray."

*Untermeyer, *Pursuit*, pp. 278-79.

170

RHYME ROYAL

This particular version of the septet is associated with King James I of Scotland. It was used with great effectiveness by Chaucer and Shakespeare, and in more recent years, by John Masefield.* Its seven lines are written in iambic pentameter with a rhyme scheme of a–b–a–b–b–c–c.**

MY LITTLE WORLD

Oh, God, I am not fit for Your great plans,
My little world is small, and so am I.
Wee babies I can hold within my hands,
And rose buds all Your wonders multiply.
Just let me live, and love, in Thee, to die,
And when the angel beckons me to go,
My poems will record the overflow.

SERENA

The ancient form of the Serena came from the medieval Provence.*** A modern adaptation into the English was devised by Edith Thompson. This intricate form requires head rhymes as well as end rhymes in the first ten lines. The eleventh line does not require rhyme. Head rhymes are in couplets. The end rhymes have a unique pattern. Lines 1 and 2 are repeated in lines 9 and 10.

WITH STARS IN MY EYES

A	I am hoping	A
A	Silently,	B
b	Scheming, though I am discreet,	c
b	Dreaming you might glance my way,	x
c	Hoping you and I can meet,	c
c	Groping to advance this feat,	c
d	Trying to attract your eye,	d
d	Sighing as you hurry by.	d
A	I am hoping	A
A	Silently	B
x	Won't you notice me?	b

*Untermeyer, *Pursuit*, p. 279, 280.
**Calkins, *Handbook*, p. 51.
***Wood, p. 66.

SESTENNELLE

This beautiful creation by Lyra LuVaile is composed of three stanzas of six lines each, and uses iambic dimeter, trimeter, and pentameter. Each stanza starts with a couplet and concludes with an inverted quatrain. The lines are centered.

FOR BOTH OF US

4	a	I walk the hills
6	a	And listen for the trills
10	b	Of your favorite birds, for memory's sake.
4	c	I watch the sea
6	c	And feel it endlessly
10	b	Advancing and retreating with my ache.
4	d	I see a rose
6	d	And wonder if it grows
10	e	Where you can see its velvet dew-kissed grace.
4	f	I hear a song,
6	f	It carries me along
10	e	Nostalgic trails that haunt me with your face.
4	g	I view the sky
6	g	And mutely wonder why
10	h	Your spirit flew away to disappear.
4	i	I feel your smile
6	i	And then it's all worthwhile.
10	h	I lived this day for both of us, my dear.

SESTET

The sestet is actually the last six lines of a sonnet. But generally a sestet can be any six-line stanza.

It may be formed by linking three couplets:*

KING OF THE HILL

a	My Persian slinks with stealthy grace
a	As if he really owns the place,
b	Observing me through amber slits,
b	While he in haughty grandeur sits,
c	And lets me know I'm lucky he
c	Will condescend to live with me.

*Untermeyer, *Pursuit*, p. 280.

A sestet may be a quatrain followed by a couplet:*

ONE CANDLE

a   One candle is a little thing,
b   But it can make my corner bright.
a   With hope aglow all fears take wing,
b   And gone are shadows of the night.
c   Thus one candle's radiant art
c   Can send a gleam from heart to heart.

A sestet may be two couplets separated by rhyming the third and sixth lines.** Shortening the "b" lines gives the form more flexibility and sprightliness.

SPACE LURE

a   Away beyond all sky and cloud
a   Beyond the path of time and shroud
b   Mysteries are,
c   Daring souls to loose the latch,
c   To leap from earth in time to catch
b   A gleaming star.

An obvious variation is to combine two sets of tercets (triplets):***

SEAGULLS

a   Tideswept footprints on the sand,
a   Mark of pirates on the land,
a   Deserted beach, their own command.
b   Discarded waste, what bill of fare,
b   A morsel here, some jetsam there,
b   Then off they fly into the air.

BURNS STANZA

Another arrangement, a–a–a–b–a–b, was used so often by Robert Burns.**** He shortened lines 4 and 6.

---

*Untermeyer, *Pursuit*, p. 280.
***Ibid.*
****Ibid.*, p. 282.
*****Ibid.*, p. 281.

OF YOU I SING

a   I love you for the things you've done,
a   Your courage, a phenomenon,
a   For struggles shared and triumphs won,
b   Of you I sing.
a   To live those days is twice the fun
b   Remembering.

For other six–line forms, see also the SESTENNELLE and the SESTINA.

SESTINA

A troubadour invention of the 13th century, the Sestina follows these rules, given in *The Complete Rhyming Dictionary and Poet's Craft Book:*[*]

- Six stanzas, each of six lines of the same length, and a concluding three–line stanza
- The lines of the six stanzas end with the same six words, not rhyming with each other unless the poet so chooses
- The arrangement of these six terminal words follows a regular law, given below
- The closing three–line stanza uses the six terminal words, three at the centers of the lines, three at the ends.

The order for the six terminal words in the six successive stanzas is as follows:

stanza one: 1, 2, 3, 4, 5, 6
stanza two: 6, 1, 5, 2, 4, 3
stanza three: 3, 6, 4, 1, 2, 5
stanza four: 5, 3, 2, 6, 1, 4
stanza five: 4, 5, 1, 3, 6, 2
stanza six: 2, 4, 6, 5, 3, 1
half stanza: 2, 4, 6
terminal words 1, 3, 5, are used near the beginning or center of the half stanza lines.

In this example the numbers refer to terminal words.

[*]Wood, pp. 84-85.

THE GYPSY HEART

God created man a living soul.   1
When Adam fell, he forfeited his rest,   2
For only peace with God would fill that need.   3
The garden barred, all that remained was hope,   4
For listening to the tempter ruined man,   5
And drove him far from Eden and from home.   6

His cage was human flesh, a transient home   6
Wherein his spirit dwelt; his life, his soul,   1
The essence of the consciousness of man,   5
Was restless now, and lonely, void of rest,   2
Aware within his reasoning of hope   4
That someday he would find his spirit's need.   3

Every son of Adam shares this need,   3
This yearning for the path that leads to home.   6
He undertakes strange detours in the hope   4
That efforts of his own would ease his soul.   1
He tries by worldly means to conjure rest,   2
To calm the gypsy heart of wandering man.   5

His clay, the body shell of fallen man   5
Asserts itself to fill the aching need   3
By keeping him too occupied to rest,   2
Too sensually involved to think of home,   6
But hollow laughter mocks the misled soul   1
Who finds no answer there, no grounds for hope.   4

(Jehovah saw the hearts which longed for hope,   4
And sent the Second Adam unto man   5
To pay the price for sin, redeem the soul   1
Of every contrite heart, who in his need   3
Gave in to love and made his heart a home   6
Where God Himself could live and be at rest.)   2

Determined once for all to end unrest   2
And finding in himself no valid hope   4
Man looked beyond to find that longed-for home,   6
That haven for the aching void in man,   5
And cried, "Oh, God, Your presence is my need,   3
Forgive my sins, and reign within my soul."   1

Cleansed is the soul, enabled now to rest;   1 2
Christ met the need, fulfilled is every hope,   3 4
Love has found man; the gypsy has come home.   5 6

SEVENELLE

This beautifully balanced new poetry form was created by Virginia Noble.* It has no fewer than two seven–line stanzas in iambic tetrameter. The last two lines of the first stanza become a refrain which is repeated as the last two lines of all stanzas. This form may be written with either masculine or feminine endings.

THE TORCH BEARER

A God-directed patient heart
Committed to the labored art
Of sifting reams of printed page
For love of Him, not paid by wage,
To capture wisdom of the age
To teach to needy searching youth
An undiluted stream of truth.

A salary is meager dole
Compared to joy within the soul
Which blesses those possessing sight
Of holy values, pure and right,
Who share the wisdom torch of light
To teach to needy searching youth
An undiluted stream of truth.

SHADORMA

This six–line free verse sentence poem authored by James Neille Northe contains the following syllable count: 3–5–3–3–7–5. Its beauty is enhanced when a strong word is used to end each line.

A DREAM ENDED

First stirrings
of a breeze turned cold
write autumn
on the leaves
of disappearing summer,
too fragile to last.

*Major Poets, Tremont, IL

SHAKESPEAREAN SONNET (See SONNET.)

SHORT METER (See Poulter's Measure, QUATRAIN.)

SONNET

The sonnet, the most popular verse form in English, covers a wide range of subjects. It contains fourteen iambic pentameter lines with a definite rhyme scheme.*

The poet compresses his ideas into an **octet** (first eight lines) and a **sestet** (last six lines), building to an effective conclusion.

PETRARCHAN SONNET

In the 14th century Petrarch established the form with such skill that his model (also called the ITALIAN and the LATIN SON-NET) continues to be widely followed. His octave presents the setting and develops the thought. His sestet provides the culminating action. The rhyme scheme of the octave is: a–b–b–a–a–b–b–a. The sestet, which usually contains three rhymes, is most commonly arranged c–d–e–c–d–e or c–d–e–e–d–c.

CHECKMATE

a	The trumpet blasts out toward the enemy,
b	Across the red-black squares its message flings
b	Its challenge with its gauntlet blusterings.
a	The pale king sets his first foot-soldier free.
a	Returning fire for fire, his strategy
b	Results in casualties as contact brings
b	A thinning of the ranks from duellings;
a	The powerful queens maneuver expertly.
c	But now the tenor changes; blood runs cold,
d	The valiant knights and rooks and bishops fall
e	In desperation trying to appease
c	The adamant dark queen's strategic hold,
d	Which leaves the challenger no hope at all —
e	The cornered helpless king drops to his knees.

MILTONIC SONNET

Using the Petrarchan rhyme scheme, the Miltonic form differs from its model in that the entire fourteen lines are molded into one unit.**

*See Wood, p. 59. See also Untermeyer, *Pursuit*, p. 285.
**Untermeyer, *Pursuit*, p. 288.

SHAKESPEAREAN SONNET

Although Shakespeare did not invent the form, he used it prolifically and effectively. It differs from the Petrarchan in structure and rhyme scheme. It is divided into three quatrains and a concluding couplet which summarizes the thought. The break between the octet and sestet is therefore less pronounced. It uses seven rhymes rather than the Petrarchan five,* as indicated in the example.

MAGIC OF AWAKENING

a	I loved you for a little while, as dew
b	On fleeting gentle moments touched with May;
a	The magic of awakening to you,
b	More fragile than a budding rose bouquet.
c	Enframed within, this vision cannot fade
d	For from its timid door my hungry eyes
c	Caught its first glimpse of why my heart was made,
d	And love was born, its ecstasy, its sighs.
e	So many friends have come and gone since then,
f	And deeper loves have blazed to feed the glow,
e	But never have I ever found again
f	The sweetness of that kiss of long ago.
g	I pick my way in secret rendezvous
g	Back through a thousand memories to you.

SPENSERIAN SONNET

Spenser's sonnet form is a compromise between the Petrarchan and the Shakespearean. It has the five rhymes of the Petrarchan model and the Shakespearean concluding couplet. The interlocking rhyme scheme has the effect of a continual flow.**

BLOW, BUGLES, BLOW!

a	Today I sensed with joy a mighty thrill
b	As eagerly I watched the marching feet
a	Of Sousa's band in perfect cadenced drill
b	Perform with pride along the festive street.
b	Their martial air performed the mystic feat
c	Of causing men to savor liberty,
b	As "Stars and Stripes Forever" swelled to greet
c	Receptive waiting citizens like me.

*Untermeyer, *Pursuit*, p. 287. See also Calkins, *Handbook*, p. 59.
**Untermeyer, *Pursuit*, p. 288. See also Calkins, *Handbook*, p. 59.

c   No watchers could respond with apathy
d   For hearts were touched, minds stirred to understand
c   The priceless heritage of being free,
d   Re-emphasized by message of the band.
e   How deep is love, beyond the how or why,
e   Engendered when Old Glory passes by.

COMPOSITE SONNET

Since the invention of the sonnet in Italy in the 13th century,* thousands and thousands of sonnets have been written. Many have been composites of other sonnet forms. Improvisation possibilities are endless in rhyme pattern and octet–sestet structure. A poet may find that he has used, for instance, the rhyming pattern of the Spenserian for his octave, and then the concluding sestet of the Petrarchan. Many of the most notable of the English sonnets are composites, including poems by Shelley and Frost. Wordsworth even wrote a celebrated composite, titled "Sonnet on the Sonnet."**

LuVAILEAN SONNET

This recent innovation of the sonnet was created by Lyra LuVaile. It uses the Shakespearean rhyming scheme and closing couplet. It is unique, however, in that lines 2, 4, 6, 8, 10, and 12 are written in dimeter.

VALLEY RENDEZVOUS

a   There is a valley waiting at the close
b   Of this life span,
a   Where every veil is lifted to expose
b   The heart of man.
c   His faith, or lack of it, will be revealed,
d   His soul laid bare,
c   With not a single secret left concealed;
d   For we must share
e   The details of our lives, its flow and shape.
f   What shall it be,
e   His judgment or His smile? There's no escape
f   For you and me.
g   If we have followed Him our lifetime through,
g   The valley then becomes a rendezvous.

*Wood, p. 62.
**Untermeyer, *Pursuit*, p. 289.

ILLINI SONNET

Invented by 20th century poet Nel Modglin, the Illini sonnet has the following rhyme scheme: a–b–c–a; b–c–d–b; c–d–e–c; e–e. It is composed in iambic meter, combining tetrameter and pentameter lines as noted. No inversions or contractions are used.*

WHAT IS A POEM?

8	Beyond all words, a mystic view,
10	An essence given shape, in phrases shared;
10	A feeling treasured from the very start
8	And captured, sparked to rendezvous
8	In lines the poet has prepared;
10	Reflecting new awareness with his art,
10	Evocative and touching the unknown;
8	Intriguing insights, framed and bared,
8	But at what cost? He gives a part
10	Of hopes, and tears, and visions of his own;
10	With artistry he shapes the overflow,
8	From tunes which well within his heart.
10	What is a poem? Who can really know
10	What bit of music makes the spirit glow?

SONNETTE

This brief American fixed form was originated by Sherman Ripley. Its seven iambic pentameter lines are rhymed a–b–b–a; c–b–c, differing just slightly from the Canopus in the rhyming scheme of its opening quatrain. It is structured to have an uninterrupted flow of verse.**

THE PRODIGAL

a	Our gypsy cat came back to us today.
b	Her whiskers trembled and her thin sides heaved
b	But we were glad to see her, so relieved
a	That she was still alive, though murky gray
c	And dirty was her coat; what teasing guile
b	Had called, this cuddly ball of fur deceived.
c	We hope that now she'll stay with us awhile.

*Modglin, p. 87.
**Wood, p. 89.

SPECIAL OCCASION POETRY (See OCCASIONAL POETRY.)

SPENSERIAN SONNET (See SONNET.)

SPENSERIAN STANZA

This form, found extensively in Spenser's *The Faerie Queen*, has been used throughout the centuries by many poets, such as Burns, Byron, Keats, Shelley, and Tennyson. Its composition is eight pentameter lines followed by one line a foot longer than the others, an **alexandrine** which is centered under the preceding eight.* Its rhyming scheme is listed.

THE MIND STAYS YOUNG

a	Youth is not a time; it is a state,
b	A state of mind conditioned by the will,
a	For confidence and hope need not abate;
b	And cheer and courage linger with us still.
b	Youth need not leave when steeper is the hill.
c	The questing soul rejuvenates the tongue,
b	And joy of living makes the heart to thrill.
c	As long as beauty lives and thanks are sung
c	The body might rebel, but yet the heart stays young.

SPORTS POETRY (See OCCASIONAL POETRY.)

STAR SEVLIN

This form designed by Lillian Mathilda Svenson is typed to form a star. Its syllable count is 4–6–8–6–8–6–4, and the rhyme scheme is a–b–b–c–a–c–a. The meter is iambic.

AT CHRISTMAS

It was foreknown
the eastern star would shine,
its rays of light and truth combine
to stir the world to wake,
and on each one its light has shown
we have the joy to make
the star our own.

*Untermeyer, *Pursuit*, p. 290. See ALEXANDRINE.

THE STELLAR

This form introduced by Viola Berg features three stanzas of eight lines each, iambic rhythm, and a combination of long and short lines. All lines are written in tetrameter except the seventh, which is written in dimeter. The fifth and sixth lines of each stanza have feminine endings. The rhyming scheme is indicated.

THE WONDER OF LITTLE THINGS

a	I do not need an Alpine crest
b	Nor awesome redwoods reigning high
a	To know that God is manifest,
b	I see Him in a butterfly.
c	I sense God's touch in starlight gleaming,
c	And in the crocus' springtime dreaming.
d	With tiny key
d	He opens doors to majesty.
e	I do not need to be aware
f	Of solar force and boundless space
e	To thrill to sunbeams in the air,
f	Each shaft a handiwork of grace.
g	Wondrous are the bluebells ringing
g	And baby hummingbirds awinging.
h	They let me know
h	A higher power made them so.
i	Each dewdrop is a diadem,
j	A miracle each emerald grass,
i	Each violet a sapphire gem,
j	Each breeze a perfume as I pass.
k	I need no thunder, driving, pounding,
k	Or roar of ocean waves resounding
l	His worth to tell —
l	God's little wonders speak so well.

THE STEPHENS

This form is named for James Stephens (1882–1950), and is patterned after the first two stanzas of his poem "The Watcher."*
It features a stanza of six short lines written in dimeter and has a unique rhyming scheme.

*Quiller-Couch, p. 1127.

THE DOOR

a	Wisdom, I seek for thee,
b	Elusive as gold.
a	Where is your latch-key?
b	Where is your hold?
x	I long to grasp
b	Your wealth to unfold.
c	I searched in the high land,
d	I scanned by the shore,
c	I dug through the sand,
d	Through skies I bore.
x	I could not find
d	Your elusive door.
e	How I longed for your food,
f	And craved for your springs.
e	Why did you elude
f	My questionings?
x	I covet the peace
f	That knowing brings.
g	I discovered your key
h	One miracle day
g	When I cried to see,
h	To find the way —
x	I found the door
h	When I knelt to pray.

THE STEVENSON

This form is patterned after "Requiem," the famous poem by Robert Louis Stevenson* (1850–1894). It has two four–line stanzas. The first three lines of each stanza rhyme with each other, and the last lines rhyme. The first three lines are composed in tetrameter, the last line is in trimeter.

*Quiller-Couch, pp. 1035-36.

OASIS

a   I have wept and grieved for the wayward child,
a   And smoothed dark places, rough and wild,
a   Attended widows, lonely-styled,
b   And sympathized by the hour.

c   I have listened to tales both sad and long,
c   Have tried to rescue right from wrong,
c   And after all this, may I sing my song
b   And search for a wildwood flower?

SWEETBRIAR

This form combining dimeter and trimeter lines is introduced by Viola Berg. Four lines in each stanza do not require rhyme, but the third and sixth rhyme with each other. Similar to the Minuette, it differs in that some lines have three poetic beats, and only one rhyme sound is used.

CORNUCOPIA

4   x   A harvest filled
4   x   With memories
6   a   Of love that will not die,
4   x   A springtime kissed
4   x   With joys and smiles,
6   a   The roses in July.

4   x   The reaping of
4   x   The golden grain,
6   a   Contentment and a sigh,
4   x   Remembrance is
4   x   A treasured gift
6   a   To comfort by–and–by.

THE SWINBURNE

This form is named for Algernon Charles Swinburne (1837–1909), and is patterned from his poem "Before the Mirror."* This graceful form features a stanza of seven lines with exact rhyming pattern. Lines 1 and 3 have feminine endings. Lines 1, 3, 5, and 6 are written in trimeter. Lines 2 and 4 are in dimeter, and line 7 is in pentameter.

*Quiller-Couch, p. 989.

AN OLD STORY

a	You came to me to borrow
b	A little song.
a	I didn't know tomorrow
b	Would prove it wrong.
c	Your spirit seemed so sad,
c	I gave the best I had;
b	My heart, naive and trusting, went along.
d	You my song expended,
e	Its tune controlled;
d	Now the music's ended,
e	Its echoes cold.
f	I should have been aware
f	To you it was a dare,
e	But I believed a story much too old.

TANKA

The Tanka is a Japanese form containing thirty-one syllables and five lines. Its first three lines are composed in strict Haiku form (see HAIKU) of 5, 7, and 5 syllables, followed by two lines of seven syllables. Like the Haiku, it is basically a compressed form of nature poetry. The Tanka has also been used for occasional poems and to express a personal lyric response. Because of its brevity, the poet can only suggest.* The imaginative reaction comes from the reader.

RAIN

5	Your tearful tongues loosed,
7	whispering of green altars
5	to reluctant skies,
7	you run before the west wind,
7	then hide in the grass, dripping.

RENGO

This Oriental verse form evolved from combining two or more Tanka.** It therefore must have at least ten lines, or multiples of five. Each grouping of five lines should conclude an area of thought. The content can be either nature poetry or man's response to it. The syllable count is 5–7–5–7–7; 5–7–5–7–7.

*Calkins, *Handbook*, p. 22
**Calkins, *Handbook*, p. 24.

EASEL ON THE BEACH

Who can frame the sea?
Could a paintbrush capture life,
the ocean's fury;
the colors on a palette
form one plunging white-capped wave?
God's wonders deserve
to be painted by the best;
yet, with awe, I try.
Critics' eyes might not approve,
but it will be my prayer.

THE TAYLOR

This form, named after Edward Taylor (1645–1729), is patterned
after his charming poem "Upon a Spider Catching a Fly."* This
form is delicately balanced with two rhymes, or approximate
rhymes, and five lines to a stanza. Line 1 has three poetic feet,
lines 2 and 4 have two, line 3 has four, and line 5 has one.

CAPTIVE FOREVER

a   If you with wit can write
b   about a fly
a   caught in a spider's web so tight,
b   then why, oh, why
b   can't I?

c   I'd really rather say
d   he left his jail,
c   but if he somehow got away,
d   to no avail
d   your tale.

e   Since you designed this pair
f   to rendezvous,
e   I'll leave the fly within your snare
f   for spider stew
f   with you.

---

*Sculley Bradley, Richmond C. Beatty, and E. Hudson Lang, eds., *The American
Tradition in Literature* (NY: W. W. Norton & Co., 1967), pp. 69-70.

THE TENNYSON

Named for Alfred, Lord Tennyson (1809–1892), this pattern is based on his poem "Ask Me No More."* The title is used as the beginning and ending words of each stanza. The body of the form is composed of three quatrains in pentameter, of which lines 1 and 4 rhyme and 2 and 3 rhyme. The title is used as a fifth line refrain and is written in dimeter.

MY LOVE FLOWS ON

a   My love flows on, beneath the mortal sight
b   Of passive eyes that look, but do not see.
b   I only know that deep inside of me
a   In channels deep and wide, yet strangely light
R   My love flows on.

c   My love flows on. It cannot stop its course
d   For it was born equipped with mystic tide,
d   Which grows and thrives and seeks you where you hide,
c   To finally immerse you with its force.
R   My love flows on.

e   My love flows on. It needs no guide nor chart
f   And pulsing forth becomes much stronger still,
f   To steal within the fences of your will
e   And tenderly surround your wary heart.
R   My love flows on.

TERCET

The tercet, or **triplet,** is a grouping of three lines which rhyme with each other.** The tercet has never been as popular as the couplet.*** In this example the three tercets have been run together without break.

*Untermeyer, *Treasury*, p. 834.
**Untermeyer, *Pursuit*, p. 294.
***Calkins, *Handbook*, p. 61.

DANDELIONS ARE

a	In my well kept neighborhood
a	Where people work the way they should
a	To keep their lawns and shrubs real good,
b	They look askance at rambling vines
b	And unpruned, carefree, windblown pines
b	And gorgeous healthy dandelions.
c	I think it's really quite a pity
c	That folk who are so smart and witty
c	Do not think my blooms are pretty.

TERCETS WITH IDENTICAL REFRAIN

A refrain used with a tercet grouping adds a desirable touch after the monotony of the rhyming. The message of the poem is emphasized and the poem is tied together.

SING ME A SONG

Sing me a song of a golden sky,
Of stars and comets blazing by,
Sing me a song of a dream and a sigh,
  Sing me a song of love.

Sing me a song of daffodils,
Of nesting birds and peaceful hills,
Of waking spring when nature thrills,
  Sing me a song of love.

Sing me a song of joys and tears,
Where happy notes drown out the fears,
And the chorus lasts a million years,
  Sing me a song of love.

TERCETS WITH VARYING REFRAIN

When a varying refrain is used, the writer has more freedom in leading into the refrain. When the final refrain is used as the title, the poem comes full circle.

CATCH A STAR FOR ME

Climb a mountain, wild and high
Where gypsy breezes laugh and cry,
And the only fence is boundless sky,
And breathe the air for me.

Feel the heartthrob of the world
Where thrilling challenges are hurled,
And wisdom is a flame unfurled,
And grasp a torch for me.

Gaze up at the purple night,
Wonder at its patterned light,
And as your spirit soars in flight,
Catch a star for me.

TERMELAY

This form, similar to the Rondelay, has a syllable count of 4–4–4–8–8–4, but has no set rhyme or meter. The third and sixth lines are identical.*

DEATH COMES UNBID

4	An opportune
4	challenge will knock;
4	death comes unbid.
8	Love coaxes, learning captivates,
8	contentment is striven for, but
4	death comes unbid.

TERZA RIMA

Literally meaning "third rhyme," the Terza Rima is composed of "a form of tercet in which the first and third lines rhyme." The rhyme in the second line is carried on by the first and third lines of the next tercet.** The interlocking rhyme arrangement can continue as long as desired.

This form can be closed by a couplet or by extending the last tercet into a quatrain. In this example the form is closed with a couplet.

---

*Fusco, "Rediscovering Verse Forms," in Calkins, Handbook, p. 25.
**Untermeyer, Pursuit, p. 295.

I NEED GREEN VALLEYS

a   I need green fertile valleys for my heart
b   Where I can get away from busy din,
a   Where faith and I can grow, so set apart
b   That hope and love will flourish deep within.
c   I want to find a quiet hallowed place
b   Where tenderness and softness will begin
c   To overcome my being, to embrace
d   A new awareness of the very earth,
c   So I will view with feeling time and space
d   And understand anew what dawn is worth,
e   To count the morning stars, watch seedlings grow,
d   And hear the feathered choirs in gales of mirth,
e   To listen to His voice, and feel the glow
e   Which only sparrows and the lilies know.

THE THORLEY

This form is patterned after the poem "Chant for Reapers" by
Wilfred Thorley (b. 1878)*. It features alternating lines of penta-
meter and trimeter, the short lines ending with feminine words.
No rhyming is used.

SURVIVAL

(The bicentennial of the landing of the pilgrims was commemorated at Plymouth on
Forefather's Day, 1820. After a memorable
address by Daniel Webster, the significance
of the five kernels of parched corn on each
plate was explained, and the perilous year of
1623 was remembered.)

Pilgrim larders pitifully low
    Required rationed sharing,
And ushered in a stoic, starving time,
    When most intense, the suffering.

However, their great faith, will to survive,
    Sustained them till the harvest,
And having weathered this, their lowest ebb,
    They lived to see the increase.

*Quiller-Couch, p. 1118.

So staggering the price these brave ones paid,
How strong, this band of outcasts,
To win against the overwhelming odds,
And will to us, their purchase.

THE TRENCH

Named after Herbert Trench (1865–1923), The Trench is patterned after his poem "A Charge."* It exhibits an interesting combination of line lengths. Lines 1, 2, and 4 are written in pentameter, line 3 is in dimeter, and line 5 in trimeter. The second
line does not require rhyme. The other lines have alternate
rhyming.

BANKRUPT

a   If on determined path pursuing gain
x   The inner man is shorn of self respect,
b   What worth is this?
a   For peace comes not from harvesting of pain,
b   Nor from a Judas kiss.

c   For when refining fire sears to assess
x   And secrets of the soul's designs are shown,
d   Then shall he see
c   The glaring consequence of barrenness,
d   Stripped of integrity.

TRIAD

This form of the triad, created by Rena Ferguson Parks, contains
three stanzas, the first and third of which have seven lines and
a refrain; the second has five lines and a refrain. Only two rhyming sounds are used, but there are a number of unrhymed lines.
All the lines are iambic tetrameter except the refrain. The refrain,
which is also the title, contains four syllables and has internal
rhyme.

*Quiller-Couch, p. 1080.

TO BE A TREE

x	My roots could stretch so far, so deep,
x	To learn the secrets of the earth,
x	My arms would reach up for the sun,
a	My branches dressed in greenery,
x	And I could play with winds that pass.
a	A life like that is worry-free.
b	A little twig can hardly wait
A	To be a tree.

x	At night the moon would share her beams,
x	In winter, snow would be my friend,
x	The rain would bathe my trunk and limbs,
a	The birds would be my company.
b	I'd be content with such a fate —
A	To be a tree.

x	And inch by inch the hill I'd claim,
x	And lift my spreading branches far,
x	A bridge between the earth and sky,
a	Where only wings and I would be.
x	Oh, you can call it what you will,
a	But when the world would gaze at me,
b	With joy I would reverberate
A	To be a tree.

This form of the triad contains three closely related ideas expressed in brief poems, with one heading and three subtitles. For example, Haiku structure was used.

MAN IS A BOUQUET

BASIC NEED

As a sunflower
needs the sun, man needs a smile,
manna for the soul.

TIME FOR TEARS

As a bleeding heart
comes into flower, so man
needs to cry sometimes.

NEED TO GIVE

As a full blown rose
is glad to spread its perfume,
so we need to share.

TRIANGLET (or Triangla)

This form by Mina M. Sutherland features an unusual shape. Its syllable count of 1–2–3–4–5–5–4–3–2–1 forms a triangle. It begins and ends with the same word, with strict rhyme scheme.

IT TAKES SPRING

A	Spring
b	awakes
c	the flowers
x	from their long sleep,
d	sends the robins north,
d	coaxes sproutings forth;
x	for mystic charm
c	and powers,
b	it takes
A	spring.

TRIBUTE POETRY (See OCCASIONAL POETRY.)

TRILINEA

This charming little form was originated by Nellie Amos. It contains three lines, of which the first and last must rhyme. Somewhere in the poem "rose" must be mentioned. Its syllable count is 4–8–4.

MEMORIES

Fragrance so frail,
pure beauty of a rose unfolds
nostalgic trail.

SOUVENIR

I am bereft;
pressed between pages is a rose,
all I have left.

TRILLIUM

Created by W. C. A. Waller, this form has five lines, with eleven syllables in lines 2, 3, and 4, which rhyme with each other. Lines 1 and 5 have only six syllables, and rhyme. Written in iambic meter, the middle lines have feminine endings and the first and last have masculine.

CAPRICCIO

The spell of night is gone,
The waves, so petulant in midnight thunder,
Scared off the moon, its splintered gleams pulled under.
Its anger spent, it isn't any wonder
The sea is calm at dawn.

TRIOLET

The Triolet is part of the Rondeau family. This brief French form uses repeat lines in a unique pattern. It has become a favorite with students because after the refrain lines have been chosen and put into place, only three lines remain to be filled in. Lines 1, 4, and 7 are the same, and line 2 is repeated in line 8.*

VIGILANTE OF THE YARD

A	Keeping watch through sun and rain,
B	Faithful scarecrow stands his guard,
a	Feeling neither joy nor pain,
A	Keeping watch through sun and rain,
a	Guardian of the seeded grain,
b	Vigilante of the yard.
A	Keeping watch through sun and rain,
B	Faithful scarecrow stands his guard.

TRIPLET (See TERCET.)

*Wood, pp. 76-77. See also Calkins, *Handbook*, p. 62.

TRIQUAIN

This form was introduced by L. Stanley Cheney. It is a three–line poem composed in the spirit of Haiku and the Cinquain, with a 2–7–7 syllable count. The first line introduces the subject and leads into the action expressed in the second line. The third line is impressionistic and can be a conclusion, a question, or a mood.*

CHARMED BY A TOUCH

Sunbeams
caress a cottage with gold;
lovelight transforms loneliness.

TROISIEME

This unique unrhymed form is composed of three groupings with syllable count of 3–5–7, plus two ending lines of nine syllables each. The first three lines introduce the subject, the next three enlarge upon it, the last three bring in a contrasting thought, and the last two lines summarize. Each line ends on a strong word.

ARTIST AT THE KEYBOARD

3	Organ tones
5	stir deep emotions,
7	playing upon heart and soul;
3	thrilling notes
5	of the meadow lark,
7	caress of the gentle rain;
3	crescendo
5	of stirring chorus,
7	deep roaring surf and thunder.
9	Expert fingers bring from mighty pipes
9	Kaleidoscope of life on parade.

*Calkins, *Handbook*, p. 63.

TULIP

This quatrain created by Viola Gardner shows unique meter combinations. The first and third lines are composed in iambic pentameter; the second contains a spondee and an amphibrach; and the fourth, an iamb and an amphibrach, with alternate rhyming. It also features internal rhyme in lines 1 and 3.* The example will illustrate that the results are simpler than the instructions suggest.

AUTUMN MOOD

I love the earth ablaze in autumn mood,
Tone tints rich glowing,
In final phase of peace and quietude
And harvest showing.

TWIN HAIKU (See HAIKU.)

UNEVEN COUPLET (See COUPLET.)

UTA

This is one of the longer very old Japanese forms which uses a delicate balance of five- and seven–syllable lines. Apostrophes are not used and strong word endings are desired. The form contains eight lines and is unrhymed.

ONLY FOR THE HEART

7	In the magic of dawning
5	prayer becomes music,
5	echoing, floating
7	through the air like cherubim
7	laughter, trailing a perfume
5	of benediction,
5	for the sweetest songs
7	of all are beyond language.

VARYING REFRAIN (See TERCETS WITH VARYING REFRAIN.)

*Calkins, *Handbook*, p. 64.

196

VELTANELLE

This form was created by Velta Myrtle Allen Sanford. It contains no more than three stanzas of six lines each, containing the following syllable count: 10–6–10–6–10–10. Lines 1, 3, 5, and 6 are in pentameter; lines 2 and 4 in trimeter. The rhyme scheme is designated at the left.

WHEN I WAS YOUNG

a	When I was young, I knew that bluebells rang,
b	Their hammers tinkling so,
a	When young, I knew the bashful breezes sang,
b	The west wind told me so.
c	I knew that kites heard music in the sky;
c	They minuetted when the clouds flew by.
d	When I was young, I knew cicadas hummed
e	A chorus just for me,
d	And friendly branches of the pine trees strummed
e	A secret melody.
f	No longer young, a new song greets my ear,
f	It waited in my heart, for me to hear.

VERS DE SOCIETE

"Society Verse" once dealt with social customs. Today it is another term for light verse.*

THE GUESSING GAME

People, people, everywhere,
Just like a bunch of ants,
A mongrel combination of
Long hair and skinny pants.
You can tell as well as I
If he's a girl, or she's a guy.

VERSO-RHYME

This form created by L. Ensley Hutton features eight lines with no punctuation but an exclamation point at the end of the stanza. It has a rhyme scheme and all line endings are aligned.

*Untermeyer, *Pursuit*, p. 300.

ALL GOD'S WONDERS WAIT

x	The hearts that feel respond
a	to candle glow
x	Are thrilled by lifted winds
b	aloft and free
x	Are touched by diamond gems
a	upon the snow
x	And all God's wonders wait
b	for you and me!

VIGNETTE

This pattern originated by Flozari Rockwood is a free verse form with six lines (twenty-six syllables), arranged 2–4–4–6–7–3. Each line ends on a strong word.*

MAGIC ART

2	Charm me
4	with your gypsy
4	spell, violin.
6	Make my stubborn heart weep.
7	Soften me, thrill me, heal me,
3	troubadour.

VILLANELLE

One of the most musical of the French forms, originally the Villa-nelle was a shepherd's song.**

  The Villanelle may be serious or frivolous. Its nineteen lines are arranged in five three–line stanzas and a concluding quatrain. The unique use of the double refrains in the structuring of this form is noted in the example. Only two rhyme sounds are used.***

LET ME BE MYSELF

A–1	My feelings, do not analyze,
b	My inner motives to assess.
A–2	Spare my soul your probing eyes.

*Calkins, *Handbook*, p. 64.
**Untermeyer, *Pursuit*, p. 301.
***Wood, p. 87.

a	Let friendship grow and exercise
b	Its own spontaneous caress,
A–1	My feelings, do not analyze.

a	Your playful baiting is unwise,
b	For hearts are not a game of chess,
A–2	Spare my soul your probing eyes.

a	Kindly do not scrutinize,
b	Apply both tact and artfulness,
A–1	My feelings, do not analyze.

a	Go, slowly, gently, I advise
b	To find the treasures I possess.
A–2	Spare my soul your probing eyes.

a	Refrain from needless ruse or guise;
b	To simple love I acquiesce.
A–1	My feelings do not analyze,
A–2	Spare my soul from probing eyes.

VIOLETTE

Another beautiful "flower-titled" form originated by Viola Gardner, this rhyming pattern contains three stanzas, each one of which is composed of a tercet, followed by a fourth line which rhymes with the fourth line of the other two verses, tying the form together. The lines are short, containing six syllables for the tercet, and four syllables for the fourth line.

EXODUS

Summer is so fleeting,
Feathered friends are meeting,
For their final greeting;
    Fall breezes blow.

Fledglings so excited,
Really quite delighted
That they were invited;
    Spirits aglow.

Signaled to be winging,
Stratosphere is ringing,
Journey starts with singing;
    Off the birds go.

VIRELET

Derived from the French Lai and the Virelay, the Virelet is of indeterminate length. The short lines of one stanza dictate the rhymes for the long lines of the succeeding stanza. To close the poem, the short lines of the last stanza rhyme with the long lines of the first stanza. The meter chosen should be used consistently. This example was written in tetrameter for lines 1 and 3, trimeter for line 2, and dimeter for line 4. Introduced by Viola Berg.

WHEN MY CRAFT EMBARKS

a	Why dread the swinging metronome,
b	Or give way to fear?
a	The light beyond the sunset gloam
b	Will soon appear.
b	Why should the path ahead seem drear?
c	Why cling to things that be?
b	There is a purer atmosphere
c	For you and me.
c	The Mighty Captain holds the key
d	To the final door.
c	I will follow hopefully
d	Trusting Him more.
d	Though the wild waves pitch and roar
a	And restless be the foam,
d	When my craft embarks on shore,
a	I will be home.

WAVELET

Originated by Marie L. Blanche Adams, this twelve–line iambic pattern alternates short-line couplets with long-line tercets in an interweaving rhyme scheme. Couplet lines have feminine endings.

ON A DAY IN MAY

5	a	The stream is dancing,
5	a	The wind is prancing,
8	b	And on this glorious day in spring,
8	c	When air is fresh and love is new,
8	b	And sunbeams kiss most everything,
5	d	When grass is greening,
5	d	And birds are preening,
8	e	When joy is rampant in the land,
8	c	And lilac buds are bursting through,
8	e	I simply cannot understand
5	f	The willow's crying,
5	f	I heard it sighing.

YAMA

This Oriental verse form is named after the ancient Hindu god of death. It contains four lines of six syllables each, with lines 2 and 4 rhyming. "The subject is usually death, but may be expanded to include grief, sorrow, or the passing of a season."*

AURA OF SPRING

The pulsing joy departs,
The spark of sonneteers,
The freshness wears away,
And magic disappears.

THE YEATS

Named after William Butler Yeats (1865–1939), this pattern is from his poem "Where My Books Go."**Lines 1, 3, 5, and 7 have feminine endings and do not require rhyme. The other four lines share the same rhyme. Trimeter is used.

*Fusco, in Calkins, *Handbook*, p. 25.
**Quiller-Couch, p. 1077.

UNDER THE LILAC TREE
(Farewell to the Family Dog)

x	We laid her in the garden
a	Where she loved to be.
x	All breath had left her body,
a	Her spirit was now free.
x	Although she rests so gently,
a	We miss her terribly.
x	She loved us even knowing
a	Our mere humanity.

ZANZE

Originated by Walden Greenwell, this sixteen–line pattern in iambic rhythm is one of the most intricate of the repeat line forms. Stanza 1 contains four eight–syllable lines. In stanza 2 the last two syllables of line 1 are dropped, and the first six are repeated. Stanza 3 starts with the first four syllables of the line, and stanza 4 begins with only the first two.

In the last stanza, line 1 is repeated as the last line, and the syllable count graduates: 2–4–6–8. The codes at the left give complete information.

GLOWING ORBIT

8	A	Beyond our sight the sun departs
8	b	And brightens other waiting lands,
8	a	Arouses minds, awakens hearts
8	b	On isles at sea, on desert sands.
6	c	Beyond our sight the sun
6	d	Fulfills its faithful rounds.
6	c	Its task is never done,
6	d	Its service knows no bounds.
4	e	Beyond our sight
4	f	To glow, to burn,
4	e	It shares its light
4	f	And will return.
2	g	Beyond
4	a	All maps or charts,
6	g	A programmed vagabond,
8	A	Beyond our sight the sun departs.

ZENITH

This form introduced by Viola Berg has a rhyming scheme but no specified line length, a feature which allows the writer freedom to expand his ideas, yet binds them neatly with rhyme. Line 1 rhymes with line 4, line 2 rhymes with line 5, line 3 with line 6, etc. Accordingly, the form should be written in units of six lines, or multiples thereof. Masculine rhyme words should be matched with masculine, and feminine with feminine.

THE PERFUME LINGERS

a	Time will not be contained
b	In vial nor shrine. Void of face
c	measureless, obscure,
a	it flows freely, unrestrained,
b	fresh, unmarred, without a trace
c	of form, geysered, pure,
d	available to make alliance
e	with, to occupy and fuse it
f	by breathing and living.
d	What a valued science,
e	to savor and use it,
f	and in giving
g	attention to the proper inventory
h	of its stewardship, thus
i	the result then exposes
g	in its final story,
h	whether weeds mastered us,
i	or if we left roses.

APPENDIX I:

HELPFUL PUBLICATIONS

The items listed are available from The Writer, Inc., (TW), or Writer's Digest (WD), at these addresses:

The Writer, Inc.
8 Arlington Street
Boston, MA 02116

Writer's Digest
9933 Alliance Road
Cincinnati, OH 45242

The Writer Magazine. A practical monthly for writers, contains timely features on all phases of writing, including the "Poet's Workshop," and up to the minute market news. (TW)

Writer's Digest Magazine. Monthly issues include timely articles, interviews, columns, tips to keep writers informed on where and how to sell their work. (WD)

Writer's Market. The bestselling hardcover annual contains more than 8,500 paying markets for novels, articles, poetry, plays, gags, short stories, and more. (WD)

Writer's Yearbook. Lots of how-to articles and special features, along with analysis of 500 major markets for non-fiction, fiction, poetry, books and cartoons. Published annually. (WD)

The Writer's Handbook, edited A. S. Burack. The standard reference book for writers; 100 chapters by leading authors, editors and teachers on fiction, non-fiction, verse, radio, TV, playwriting, etc. Plus up-to-date lists of over 2,500 markets for manuscript sales. Tells what to write, how to write, where to sell. New edition. (TW)

The Writer's Rhyming Dictionary, by Langford Reed. A valuable and complete list of rhymes, arranged alphabetically. Introduction gives instruction for poets. (TW)

The Poet and the Poem, by Judson Jerome. A comprehensive look at both the art and the craft of poetry, with lively discussions of diction, meter, rhyme, sound texture, meaning, inspiration — and publication. Revised edition. (WD)

Writing a Poem, by Florence Trefethen. Instruction in writing poetry — planning, writing, and revision. (TW)

Writing Poetry, by John Holmes. An important and helpful book about the poet's work by a well-known poet and teacher of poetry writing. (TW)

First Principles of Verse, by Robert Hillyer. A handbook on fundamental elements of verse — diction, imagery, meter, form, and bases of criticism. (TW, WD)

Selling Poetry, Verse, and Prose, by Carl Goeller. Advice on writing and selling to greeting card and magazine markets. Lists markets and describes "idea wheel." (TW)

The Greeting Card Writer's Handbook, edited H. Joseph Chadwick. Former editor of a leading greeting card company tells how to get ideas for cards that sell. Newly revised. (WD)

Sound and Sense, by Laurence Perrine. For the student of poetry, this is an excellent introduction to poetry, particularly good on figurative language and imagery, the relationship of sound to sense, and differentiating good from great poetry. Third edition. Available from the publisher, Harcourt, Brace and Jovanovich.

World Poetry Society, Dr. Mabelle A. Lyon, Chancellor, 8801 N. 17th Ave., Phoenix, AZ 85021.

COLLEGE AND UNIVERSITY PUBLICATIONS

Arizona Quarterly, University of Arizona, Tucson, AZ 85721.
Boston University Journal, West Tower Three, 775 Commonwealth Ave., Boston, MA 02115.
The California Quarterly, 100 Sproul, University of California, Davis, CA 95616.
Chicago Review, The University of Chicago, Faculty Exchange Box C, Chicago, IL 60637.
Dark Tower Magazine, Cleveland State University, University Center, Cleveland, OH 44115.
Denver Quarterly, University of Denver, Denver, CO 80210.
Descant, Dept. of English, Texas Christian University, Fort Worth, TX 76129.
Event, c/o Douglas College, Box 2503, New Westminster B.C., Canada.
Everyman Magazine, 2900 Community College, Cleveland, OH 44115.
Firelands Arts Review, Firelands Campus, Huron, OH 44839.
Florida Quarterly, 330 J.U. Reitz Union, University of Florida, Gainesville, FL 32601.
Four Quarters, LaSalle College, Olney Ave. at 20th St., Philadelphia, PA 19141.
From the Hills, Morris Harvey College, Charleston, WV 25304.
The Great Lakes Review, Northeastern Illinois University, Chicago, IL 60625.
Hawaii Review, Hemenway Hall, University of Hawaii, Honolulu, HI 96822.
Jeopardy, Viking Union, Western Washington State College, Bellingham, WA 98225.
Kansas Quarterly, Dept. of English, Kansas State University, Manhattan, KS 66502.
Karamu, English Dept., Eastern Illinois University, Charleston, IL 61920.
The Lake Superior Review, Box 724, Ironwood, MI 49938.
The Literary Review, Fairleigh Dickinson University, Rutherford, NJ 07070.
The Midwest Quarterly, Kansas State College, Pittsburgh, KS 66762.
New Orleans Review, Loyola University, New Orleans, LA 70118.
Nimrod, University of Tulsa, 600 Woth College, Tulsa, OK 74104.
The North American Review, University of Northern Iowa, Cedar Falls, IA 50613.
Northwest Review, University of Oregon, Eugene, OR 97403.
Occident, Eshleman Hall, Berkeley, CA 94720.
The Ohio Review, Ellis Hall, Ohio University, Athens, OH 45701.
Perspectives, English Dept., West Virginia University, Morgantown, WV 26506.

The Phoenix, Morning Star Farm, West Whately, RFD Haydenville, MA 01039.

Pigiron, Pigiron Press, P.O. Box 237, Youngstown, OH 44501.

Prairie Schooner, Andrews Hall, University of Nebraska, Lincoln, NB 68508.

Riverside Quarterly, Box 14451, University Station, Gainesville, FL 32604.

Roanoke Review, Roanoke College, Salem, VA 24153.

The Seneca Review, Hobart and William Smith Colleges, Geneva, NY 14456

Sewanee Review, University of the South, Sewanee, TN 37375.

The South Carolina Review, Dept., of English, Clemson University, Clemson, SC 29631.

South Dakota Review, Box 11, University Exchange, Vermillion, SD 57069.

The Southern Review, Drawer D, University Station, Baton Rouge, LA 70803.

Southwest Review, Southern Methodist University, Dallas, TX 75275.

Spectrum, University of Massachusetts, Student Union, R.S.O. 102, Amherst, MA 01002.

Texas Quarterly, Box 7517, University Station, Austin, TX 78712.

Thought, The Quarterly of Fordham University, Fordham University Press, Box L, Fordham University, The Bronx, NY 10458.

*Twigs,*College Box 2, Pikeville College, Pikeville, KY 41501.

Western Humanities Review, University of Utah, Salt Lake City, UT 84112.

ACKNOWLEDGMENTS I:

ORIGINATORS AND THEIR PATTERNS

Abercrombie, Lascelles. THE ABERCROMBIE.
Adams, Marie L. Blanche. ADAGEM, BREVEE, KERF, SCALLOP, WAVELET.
Allinder, Thelma. BRAGI.
Amos, Nellie. TRILINEA.
Armstrong, Etheree. ETHEREE.
Arnold, Matthew. THE ARNOLD.
Barkan, Stanley H. APOSTROPHE.
Bentley, Edmund Clerihew. CLERIHEW.
Berg, Viola Jacobson. AFFLATUS, BRIOLETTE, THE DONNA, THE HAUTT, THE LAUREL, THE LOUISE, MARIANNE, MINUETTE, PALETTE, THE STELLAR, SWEETBRIAR, ZENITH.
Binyon, Laurence. THE BINYON.
Blunden, Edmund. THE BLUNDEN.
Boyce, Monica. CHAIN LANTERNE.
Braden, Eve. DORSIMBRA.
Bridges, Robert. THE BRIDGES.
Bryant, William Cullen. THE BRYANT.
Caldwell, Robert. HOURGLASS.
Cary, Robert. CARYOTTE.
Cheney, L. Stanley. TRIQUAIN.
Crapsey, Adelaide. CINQUAIN.
Cunningham, Ella M. CADENCE.

De La Mare, Walter. THE DE LA MARE.
De Tabley, John Leicester Warren, Lord. THE DETABLEY.
Dewey, Mildred Nye. DUNI.
Dickson, Margaret Ball. DICKSON NOCTURNE, MINIATURE.
Dixon, Richard Watson. THE DIXON.
Dobson, Henry Austin. THE DOBSON.
Donne, John. THE DONNE.
Dorris, Frieda . DORSIMBRA.
Dowson, Ernest. THE DOWSON.
Evans, Lucille. ARABESQUE.
Fishback, Jessamine. SAN HSIEN.
Fletcher, John. THE FLETCHER.
Freeman, Olivia. FRIEZE (DICKSEE).
Gardner, Viola. AMARANTH, FIALKA, FOR–GET–ME–NOT, GARDE-
NIA, LADY'S SLIPPER, TULIP, VIOLETTE.
Gilbert, William Schwenk. THE GILBERT.
Gray, James R. DR. STELLA, NEVILLE.
Greenwell, Walden. ZANZE.
Hartwich, Ethelyn Miller. QUINNETTE.
Herrick, Robert. THE HERRICK.
Hutton, L. Ensley. LYRA CHORD, RIPPLE ECHO, VERSO–RHYME.
Kahn, Hannah. CAVATINA.
Kaye, Gee. HEXADUAD.
Kipling, Rudyard. THE KIPLING.
LuVaile, Lyra. QUINTANELLE, SEPTANELLE, SESTENELLE,
LUVAILEAN SONNET.
Merrell, Lloyd Frank. LANTERNE.
Mellichamp, Ina. CROSS LIMERICK.
Miller, Paul Emile. CYCLE.
Miller, Queena Davison. ARKAHAM BALLAD.
Modglin, Nel. LAVELLE, MANARDINA, ILLINI SONNET.
Murphy, Etta J. PENDULUM.
Murrell, E. Ernest. BACCRESEIZE, CINQUETUN.
Newman, Israel. LYRETTE.
Noble, Fay Lewis. QUINTETTE.
Noble, Virginia. SEVENELLE.
Northe, James Neille. CINQUINO, SHADORMA.
Noyes, Alfred. THE NOYES.
Nutter, Joseph N. DECANNELLE.
O'Donnell, Dion. DIONOL.
O'Shaughnessy, Arthur William Edgar. THE O'SHAUGHNESSY.
Parks, Rena Ferguson. ANALOGUE, CIRCLET, TRIAD.
Pendleton, Anne. DECATHLON.
Phelps, Elizabeth Maxwell. SEAFONN.
Phillimore, John Swinnerton. THE PHILLIMORE.
Ripley, Sherman. SONNETTE.
Rockwood, Flozari. LOGOLILT, RETOURNELLO, VIGNETTE.

Russell, George William. THE RUSSELL.
Sanford, Velta Myrtle Allen. LYRELLE, VELTANELLE.
Simonton, Robert. DORSIMBRA.
Sipfle, Louise. TWIN HAIKU.
Smith, Ann Byrnes. BOUTONNIERE, SEOX.
Smither, John Milton. METRIC PYRAMID.
Spokes, Alice Maude. CAMEO, PENSEE.
Stephens, James. THE STEPHENS.
Stevenson, Robert Louis. THE STEVENSON.
Sutherland, Mina M. TRIANGLET.
Svenson, Lillian Mathilda. MEDALLION, OCTAIN, STAR SEVLIN.
Swinburne, Algernon Charles. ROUNDEL, THE SWINBURNE.
Taylor, Edward. THE TAYLOR.
Tennyson, Alfred, Lord. THE TENNYSON.
Thompson, Edith. MARGEDA, SERENA.
Thorley, Wilfred. THE THORLEY.
Tompkins, Dora. DUODORA.
Trench, Herbert. THE TRENCH.
Waller, W.C.A. TRILLIUM.
Winsett, Marvin Davis. THE CYCLUS.
Yeats, William Butler. THE YEATS.

ACKNOWLEDGMENTS II:

PUBLICATIONS IN WHICH POEMS IN THIS BOOK HAVE APPEARED

The American Bard, Hollywood, CA: THE GUESSING GAME, as "Identification"; MY LOVE FLOWS ON; WRITER'S DILEMMA

American Greetings, Cleveland, OH: MAGIC OF AWAKENING

American Poet, Charleston, IL: BOOMERANG; A WISHING STAR

American Poetry League Bulletin, Charleston IL: MAGIC OF A SUNBEAM; TO SOAR ALOFT

American Poets Fellowship Society, Charleston, IL: "Great Concepts Contest," 1971, first place winner: TO SEE THE LIGHT, as "To Find the Light"

American Voice, Charleston, IL: SING ME A SONG

The Angel Hour, Campbell, CA: MAN IS A BOUQUET, as "Lesson of the Flowers"; ONLY FOR THE HEART; TO THOSE WHO ASK

The Angels, Central Islip, NY: WITH GIANT HAND

Anthology of the Flowers, Barry, TX: SAGA OF THE FLOWERS, as "Ballad of the Flowers"

Arkadelphia News, Arkadelphia, AR: GHOSTS WHO NEVER DIE

Author-Poet, Birmingham, AL: BENEDICTION; MAN IS A BOUQUET, as "Lesson of the Flowers"

Conzoni, Beaumont, CA: AGELESS

Country World Magazine, Carmi, IL: THEY MET THEIR GOD, as "Through the Snow"; WILD OATS OR PUMPKINS, as "As We Sow"; Willie died . . . ; Willie's brother . . .

Cranston Herald, Providence, RI: SOLDIERS ON THE ROOF

Cyclo-Flame, San Angelo, TX: ANOTHER DAY UNFOLDS; DEATH COMES UNBID, as "No Invitation"

Delight Magazine, Austin, TX: ARTIST AT THE KEYBOARD

Encore Magazine, Albuquerque, NM: INDIAN SUMMER

Essence, Brookville, NY: ESSENCE

The Explorer, South Bend, IN: SMALLER THAN A MUSTARD SEED

Fellowship in Prayer, New York, NY: MORNING STAR OF DAY, as "As Panteth Yet the Hart"

Fine Arts Discovery Magazine, Kansas City, MO: SKY BALLET

Firefly, Redwood Falls, MN: EXODUS; GRIST FOR THE WASTEBASKET; THE SILENT SPY

Flamingo, Miami Beach, FL: A CUP OF WATER; LOVE IS ALL THE TIME; MAGIC OF AWAKENING; A POEM IS BORN; THE TEARS ARE SINGING; TWO MASTERS

For Kindred Hearts: A chronic fault-finder was Chedder; A FINE KETTLE OF FISH; THE PAUSE THAT PAYS; UNDERSTANDING GAP

Good News, Elgin, IL: THE BREAD OF LIFE

The Good Old Days, Danvers, MA: CORNUCOPIA

Great Ideals Anthology, American Poets Fellowship Society, Charleston, IL: TO KEEP OUR BROTHER

The Greatness of God, Fennville, MI: SNATCHING SPLINTERS, as "Remove the Beam"

The Guild, Idaho Falls, ID: THE GREATEST OF ALL

Harbor Lights, Shoreview, MN: UPON OUR DOORSTEP

Harvest of the Heart: CORNUCOPIA; THE LITTLE COUNTRY THINGS; THE PERFUME LINGERS; SOFT AS A WHISPER

The Heart of Things: BALLAD BISCUITS, as "Husband's Lament"; CEASE FIRE, as "Truce"; DANDELIONS ARE, as "Point of View"; GOD OF THE SPARROW; KING OF THE HILL; SMALLER THAN A MUSTARD SEED

The Heavenly Angels Anthology, Los Angeles, CA: BY THE FLICK OF A FINGER, as "According to Plan"

Hoosier Challenger, Cincinnati, OH: MEMORIES

Ideals, Milwaukee, WI: THE LITTLE COUNTRY THINGS

Inky Trails, Nampa, ID: ABANDONED; BALLAD BISCUITS, as "Husband's Lament"; BLOW, BUGLES, BLOW!; I NEED GREEN VALLEYS, as "The Quiet Heart"; WHEN MY CRAFT EMBARKS, as "Journey of Faith"

Jean's Journal, Kanona, NY: COME, FLY WITH ME: LITTLE BOY LOST

Joyous Hearts, Barry, TX: HOW CAN WE DOUBT

Kansas Kernels, Valley Center, KS: AN HOUR IN MY HAND, as "Temporary Custody"

Ladies Delight, Houston, TX: ONE CANDLE

L. I. Writers Newsletter, Oyster Bay, NY: BLOW, BUGLES, BLOW!; "OVER THIRTY" LAMENT; TO A TEDDY BEAR

L. I. Writers 1969 Annual: IN CLOUD OR CALM, as "He Knows the Way"

The Lincoln Herald, Harrogate, TN: BOND OF GRIEF

Maize This Week, Valley Center, KS: MONARCH OF THE NIGHT

Major Poets, Charleston, IL: THE LITTLE COUNTRY THINGS; UNDER THE LILAC TREE, as "Farewell to Buffy"

Major Poets, Tremont, IL: OCTOBER WOODS; A SLUGGARD AT HEART

The Malverne Herald, Malverne, NY: CAPTIVE FOREVER; GOD OF THE SPARROW; KING OF THE ROAD

The Malverne Times, Malverne, NY: A FINE KETTLE OF FISH; THE HEART-TUG OF YOU

Merlin's Magic, Brooklyn, NY: SOUVENIR

Midwest Chaparral, Denver, CO: GRAVEYARD OF DREAMS; INNER SANCTUM, as "Aspiration"; TO SING ANOTHER DAY, as "The Source of Power"

Midwest Chaparral, Kansas City, KS: HEADSTONE FOR THE OLD WEST

Model-T Ford Club, Bakersfield, CA: KING OF THE ROAD

The Muse, Monticello, AR: ODE TO WILLIAM SHAKESPEARE

The Muse, Newburg, OR: FACES OF RESPECT; GUN SHY; INDEPENDENCE DAY PARADE

The Muse, Cathlamet, WA: GOODNIGHT, WITH LOVE; LET THERE BE LIGHT; A POET SINGS OF LITTLE THINGS

Mustang Review, Denver, CO: TEPEES IN THE TWILIGHT

New Poetry, Charleston, IL: CHECKMATE

1969 Anthology of New York Poets, Thom Hendricks Associates, Birmingham, AL: OASIS

The Nutmegger, Danbury, CT: INFINITY; MY LOVE FLOWS ON; SAGA OF THE FLOWERS, as "Ballad of the Flowers"

Painted Poetry Appreciations, Tuskegee Institute, AL: TO SING ANOTHER DAY, as "The Source of Power"

Phyllis Magazine, Rocky Hill, CT: MIRACLE OF THE RAIN; PARADE OF THE HOURS

The Piggott Times, Piggot, AR: THE SILENT SPY

Pixie Angel, Los Angeles, CA: PEACE FOR THE HEART

Poet, Urbana, IL: DEVOURED BY A LION, as "Vanity, Thy Name Is Blind"

The Poetry Corner, Lovely, KY: BUT I MUST TRY; MY BIT OF SKY; THE PRICE OF HARVEST

Poetry Highlights, Russell, KY: IT'S FUN TO DREAM

Poetry Society of Kentucky, "Religious Category Contest," 1971, first place: THE WONDER OF LITTLE THINGS

The Poetry Society of New Hampshire, Manchester, NH: PERFUME OF A MEMORY

The Poet's Corner, Los Angeles, CA: GOD OF THE SPARROW

Poet's Party Line, Hot Springs, AR: ON SUCH A NIGHT

Prairie Poet, Charleston, IL: SUNRISE TO SUNSET, as "Energy of Light"; WHEN I HAVE GONE

Quintessence, Shreveport, LA: MAN IS JUST A DOT, as "From the Heart"

Rhythmic Bard Beats, Tooele, UT: A TREE IS A FRIEND; WHERE ARE THE JUBILANT?, as "A Soldier's Mother Speaks"

The Saint, Brooklyn, NY: ANGEL SONG; DANDELIONS ARE, as "Point of View"

Shades of Thought, Greenway, AR: FEATHERED REQUIEM

Southern Standard, Arkadelphia, AR: AURA OF SPRING, as "Spell of Spring"; PARADE OF THE HOURS

Sparkling Gems, Barry, TX: I BELIEVE; SYMPATHY BECOMES A CROWN, as "The Path to Sympathy"

The Star of Hope, El Monte, CA: JOURNEY OF A MOTHER; NEVER A SUNSET, as "The Last Journey"

Sunburst, Miami Beach, FL: APRIL BONNET

Tempo, Windsor, Ont., Canada: INFINITY

The Texas Clarion,Wichita Falls, TX: STAMPEDE OF THE LONG HORNS

Time to Pause, Nampa, ID: THE GOD WHO CANNOT DIE

Triangle, Flint, MI: SEAGULLS

Tumblin' Weeds, Wichita, KS: TRAIL OF HEALING

United Amateur Poets, Silver Springs, MD: THE CYCLE

United Amateur Poets, Roanoke, VA: TALE OF A COWARD; TRAIL OF HEALING

United Amateur Poets Association, Findlay, OH: LET ME BE MYSELF

United Poets, Charleston, IL: CATCH A STAR FOR ME; THE PERFUME LINGERS

Verdure, Oyster Bay, NY: FORT GORDON, U.S.A., as "The Precision Machine"; HER NAME IS EVE, as "Temptation"; PERFUME OF A MEMORY; THE PRICE OF HARVEST

The Villager, Bronxville, NY: APRIL BONNET; FOR BOTH OF US

Vision, St. Louis, MO: KING OF THE HILL

Wings of Good Tidings: A CHANCE TO LOVE, as "By Invitation Only"

World Poets, Charleston, IL: LIFE IS A RHYTHM

218

BIBLIOGRAPHY

Aldington, Richard, editor. *The Viking Book of the English Speaking World.* New York: The Viking Press, 1958, vol. 1.

Bailey, Temple, in "Food for Thought," reprinted in *Streams in the Desert,* compiled by Mrs. Charles E. Cowman. Grand Rapids, MI: Zondervan Publishing House, 1966.

Bradley, Sculley; Richmond C. Beatty; and E. Hudson Lang, editors. *The American Tradition in Literature.* New York: W.W. Norton & Co., Inc., 1967.

Calkins, Jean, compiler. *Handbook on Haiku and Other Form Poems.* Kanona, NY: J & C Transcripts, 1970.

Calkins, Jean, editor. *Jean's Journal.* Kanona, NY: J & C Transcripts, Spring 1969, Summer 1969, Autumn 1969, Spring 1970, February–March 1971, June–July 1971, October–November 1971.

Calkins, Jean, editor. *Haiku Highlights.* Kanona, NY: J & C Transcripts, November 1968, July–August 1970, September–October 1970.

Harr, Lorraine Ellis, editor. *Dragonfly.* Kanona, NY: J & C Transcripts, July 1976.

Marks, Mary E., editor. *Major Poets.* Hot Springs National Park, AR, Spring 1975.

Modglin, Nel. *The Rhymer and Other Helps for Beginning Poets.* Kanona, NY: J & C Transcripts, 1975.

Page, Curtis Hadden, editor. *The Chief American Poets.* New York: Houghton, Mifflin & Co., 1905.

Preminger, Alex, editor. *Encyclopedia of Poetry and Poetics*. Princeton, NJ: Princeton University Press, 1965.

Quiller-Couch, Sir Arthur, editor. *The Oxford Book of English Verse*. New York: Oxford University Press, 1941.

Untermeyer, Louis. *The Pursuit of Poetry*. New York: Simon and Schuster, 1969.

Untermeyer, Louis, compiler. *A Treasury of Great Poems*. New York: Simon and Schuster, 1942.

Webster's Third New International Dictionary. Springfield, MA: G & C Merriam Co., 1968.

Webster's Seventh New Collegiate Dictionary. Springfield, MA: G & C Merriam Co., 1963.

Wood, Clement, editor. *The Complete Rhyming Dictionary and Poet's Craft Book*. Garden City, NY: Doubleday & Co., 1936.

INDEX I: TITLES,

BY PATTERN AND PAGE

*Upper case designates poem title; lower case designates first line, untitled poem.

INDEX II:

PATTERNS, TOOLS, TERMS